How to Administer a Florida Trust

A Guide for New Trustees, as well as Trust Creators and Beneficiaries

Prepared for the public by
J. Mark Fisher, a Florida Trust Attorney

How to handle the paperwork • Who to call to get things done
What information is needed • When to call the lawyer for help

www.jmarkfisher.com

Published by J. Mark Fisher

ISBN: 978-0-9770262-1-0

Printed in Pensacola, FL.

Before We Begin—Read This First

To the Trustee of a Trust:

Taking on the job as a Trustee or successor Trustee after someone has died is a major responsibility. This Guide will give you the tools and information you need to put you immediately in the driver's seat. You will know what to do, where to go, and what information you are required to provide to any beneficiaries. You will be able to identify assets controlled by the Trust and assets not controlled by the Trust. With each step along the way, you will be guided on what you can do as the Trustee and when you need to hire expert help. Most help will come from the estate planning lawyer who helped prepare the documents. Other expert help may come from a CPA or real estate agent or appraiser.

The goal of this Guide is to allow you to quickly and efficiently do your job but keep you out of legal trouble. There will be many times as you move through the Trust administration process, where you will be instructed to "GET AN ATTORNEY." This means you have reached a point involving issues you cannot resolve yourself, where the legal issues are such that you will find yourself in court in big trouble and may be facing personal financial responsibility if you do not obtain legal counsel.

To the beneficiary of a Trust:

If a bank, brokerage firm or attorney's office has been named as Trustee, the Trust administration process should progress smoothly. There are exceptions to this rule, however, but it is much easier to hold them accountable than one of your own siblings. Just remember that yours is not the only Trust they may be administering and that they generally operate efficiently, trying at all times to avoid problems and potential litigation.

If your sibling or other family member has been named as Trustee of your parents' Trust, you should expect them to perform the duties and responsibilities described in this Guide. If you find they are not performing those duties and responsibilities as they are supposed to, you should seek your own independent legal counsel and, if need be, force them to administer the Trust appropriately.

You may be entitled to have your legal counsel paid for by the Trust, or, under severe circumstances, by the brother or sister administering the Trust from his or her own pocket.

Be aware, there is a timeline of activities to complete in administering the Trust. Although a Trust distribution can be made quickly, sometimes it takes many months to sort out the assets, liabilities and beneficiary issues. (So do not buy a new car until the check clears the bank.)

To the parent creating a Trust:

Many parents agonize over the selection of the Trustee for their family Trust. They do not want to show favoritism. However, after reviewing the duties and responsibilities described here, it is always best to select the child or other family member most capable of getting the job done well. Your choice does not have to be the child with the most business sense but the one who is fair and honest, and who will faithfully follow the steps to administer your estate according to the terms you have set forth in the Trust. One final cautionary word: never, ever, select two children to act jointly as Co-Trustees.

DISCLAIMER

This book was written by J. Mark Fisher, Attorney at Law, and is for informational purposes only. It is not meant to be legal advice nor should any part be taken as providing legal advice. The descriptions and excerpts of laws found in this book are provided for instructional purposes only and should not be taken, or used as, the basis for making any legal decision. An attorney should always be consulted for legal advice regarding the application of these or any laws to any individual situation. Further, the laws of specific jurisdictions may vary.

The staff of J. Mark Fisher, Attorneys at Law, is composed of experienced, knowledgeable, and caring individuals who are dedicated to offering probate and Trust administration services statewide. If you would like to engage the services of our firm to help with a Trust administration, please call our office at 850-244-8989 or visit our website at www.jmarkfisher.com.

The hiring of a lawyer is an important decision. Before you decide, ask us to send you free written information about our qualifications and experience.

ACKNOWLEDGMENT

I would like to thank Tammy Q. Reynolds for editing and reviewing the book. She has been employed at my office for more than 11 years, and now works remotely from New Zealand.

Contents

Part One - The Trust Administration Process 1

A. First Stage of Trust Administration: Gathering the Facts........ 1
B. Second Stage of Trust Administration: Managing the Assets 13
C. Third Stage of Trust Administration: County Filings, Tax Documents and Probate 21
D. Fourth Stage of Trust Administration: Final Accounting and Distribution 27
E. Problems 33
F. Boring but Important Legal Stuff 51

Part Two - Trusts 57

A. The Living Revocable Trust: Definitions, How They Work, How to Fund Them, and What Happens if they are Not Properly Funded........ 57
B. Other Types of Trusts........ 75

Part Three – Appendix of Example Forms 85

Figure 1 Trustee Acceptance 87

Figure 2 IRS-Form SS-4 (Application for Employer Identification Number) 88

Figure 3 Third Party Authorization 89

Figure 4 Certification of Trust 90

Figure 5 Request to Open Safe-Deposit Box........ 92

Figure 6 Notice of Trust 93

Figure 7 Trustee Letter to Beneficiary 94

Figure 8 Trust Inventory........ 95

Figure 9 Affidavit of No Florida Estate Tax Due 96

Figure 10 Affidavit of Continuous Marriage 97

Figure 11 IRS Form 56 (Notice Concerning Fiduciary Relationship) 98

Figure 12 IRS Form 4810 (Request for Prompt Assessment Under Internal Revenue Code Section 6501(d)) 100

Figure 13 IRS Form 5495 (Request for Discharge From Personal Liability Under Internal Revenue Code Section 2204 or 6905) 101

Figure 14 Trustee's Proposed Plan of Distribution 102

Figure 15 Partial Receipt and Release and Refunding Agreement 103

Figure 16 Waiver of Annual/Final Accounting 104

Figure 17 Trustee's Accounting 105

Figure 18 No Objection to Annual/Final Accounting 112

Figure 19 Final Waiver, Receipt, Release and Refunding Agreement 113

Part One - The Trust Administration Process

A. First Stage of Trust Administration: Gathering the Facts

- ☐ 1. Locate the original Trust documents, including all amendments and the original Pour-Over Will.
- ☐ 2. Review provisions regarding the distribution of the Trust and the duties of the Trustee.
- ☐ 3. Sign Trustee Acceptance Form.
- ☐ 4. Obtain a new Tax Identification Number.
- ☐ 5. Sign Certification of Trust.
- ☐ 6. Obtain certified death certificates.
- ☐ 7. Open safe-deposit box.
- ☐ 8. File original Pour-Over Will with clerk of the court in county where decedent lived.
- ☐ 9. Change address at the Post Office.
- ☐ 10. File Notice of Trust.
- ☐ 11. Review the named beneficiaries and compare them to the interested parties.
- ☐ 12. Determine if the surviving spouse has waived their rights under Florida Statute.
- ☐ 13. Obtain new Tax Identification Numbers for any continuing Trusts, such as a Special Needs Trust or Grandchildren's Trust.
- ☐ 14. Send statutorily required beneficiary letter and make copies of all Trust documents, including all amendments, and send them by certified mail to beneficiaries.

1. Locate the original Trust documents, including all amendments and the original Pour-Over Will.

It is important to locate the original Trust document, any amendments, and the original Pour-Over Will. (Most Trust packages contain what is called a Pour-Over Will, which appoints a person to be the Personal Representative of the estate and names the Trust as the sole beneficiary of any probate estate. Any asset that is left in the decedent's name only, without a designated beneficiary, will require action by the probate court.) Many attorneys today have all of their estate documents signed with blue ink making it easier to identify the original documents. Many banks and brokerage firms may want to see the original document and then make copies from it. In the alternative, they may want an attorney to certify he or she has reviewed the original document and this is a true and correct copy of it. A copy can be used if the original cannot be located. However, there may be concerns regarding why the original cannot be located. It is possible the Trust maker changed their mind or created an amendment to the original document.

The person appointed as successor Trustee should review the Trust to make sure it has not been altered or tampered with. Examples include new or retyped pages placed in the document. We have seen cases where the print type changes from one page to the next, which would indicate a new page has been inserted. If the page numbering is off, or the paper appears to be different, or if the Trust document just appears questionable in any way, you need to consult legal counsel immediately.

2. Review provisions regarding the distribution of the Trust and the duties of the Trustee.

Before going any further, the person appointed as successor Trustee will want to thoroughly review the documents and become aware of how involved the administration of the Trust will be. Some Trusts simply distribute all assets to the named beneficiaries outright and free of Trust, while others may hold the share for one or more beneficiaries for their benefit for a specific time period. A continuing Trust may mean a lengthy and more time consuming commitment for the Trustee, depending on the circumstances. The Trust may give specific gifts or powers to a named beneficiary, it may forgive an existing debt, or it may state a beneficiary's share is to be reduced by money given by the Trustor during their lifetime.

People often find themselves overwhelmed by the language used in legal documents. Not only are some of the terms unique and specific to the field of law, some are literally in a different language. Below is a list and description of commonly used terms a Trustee may need to be familiar with in order to understand the distribution:

- ***Advancement*** — A gift of money or property made by a Trustor while living to a beneficiary. The value of the gift shall be deducted from the beneficiary's share of the estate after the Trustor's death.

- ***Bequest*** — A bequest is a gift of personal property owned by a decedent at the time of death which is directed by the provisions of the decedent's Trust or Will. A bequest may include, but not be limited to, money, stocks, bonds, household items or jewelry.

- ***Devise*** — A devise is a gift of real property owned by a decedent at the time of death which is directed by the provisions of the decedent's Trust or Will.

- ***Per Capita*** — A Latin phrase that means by heads. Each living named beneficiary receives an equal share. If a beneficiary predeceases the Trustor, their share lapses and is not distributed to their heirs.

- ***Per stirpes*** — A Latin phrase that means by roots or stocks or representation. If a beneficiary predeceases the Trustor, the beneficiary's share of the inheritance will go to the beneficiary's children.

The Trust should also be reviewed for additional duties or specific instructions for the Trustee. The Trust might limit the Trustee's ability to settle disputes, or it may determine who is, and who is not, allowed to access the homestead property. The Trust document may require the Trustee to obtain a bond before beginning the administration or may give the Trustee broad discretion regarding the distribution of certain funds. If the Trustee has any questions regarding the distribution of the Trust or the provisions for the Trustee, they should consult a licensed Florida attorney.

If after these reviews, the person appointed as successor Trustee decides that he or she does not want to accept the appointment because of the nature of the duties and responsibilities that will be involved with the Trust, they should notify the appropriate parties and decline the position in writing.

3. Sign Trustee Acceptance Form.

Once the person appointed as successor Trustee decides to accept the role, he or she should sign a Trustee Acceptance Form in order to announce the decision legally. (See Figure 1 for a sample Acceptance Form.) Simply being named is not enough as the Trustee has the right to decline the appointment. Financial institutions will want to know the Trustee has accepted the position. In accepting to serve as Trustee, an individual is agreeing to administer the Trust in accordance with the Florida Trust Code and will be held to the same standard as a bank Trustee. Fla. Stat. § 736.0813(1)(a) requires the Trustee to notify the qualified beneficiaries of his or her acceptance within 60 days.

4. Obtain a new Tax Identification Number.

Prior to death, the decedent's Social Security number was the tax identification number for the Trust. (This number is also referred to as the Employer Identification Number (EIN).) After death, the decedent's Social Security number can no longer be used, and a new number must be obtained. IRS Form SS–4 is used to obtain this new identification number, and an example form is shown in Figure 2. The form can be sent to the IRS or completed online. Once the application is processed, the IRS will issue a new tax identification number. (If done online, the number may be issued within minutes.) This number will be used on every bank account, brokerage account and on any final tax returns for the estate. It is <u>never</u> appropriate for the successor Trustee's Social Security number to be used as the Trust identification number.

The Trustee can complete this form themselves, or they can fill in a Third Party Authorization Form (see Figure 3 for an example form) which allows a third party to obtain the employer identification number online for them. The SS-4 Form will be completed along with this authorization allowing the third party to submit the application online.

5. Sign Certification of Trust.

Fla. Stat. § 736.1017 allows the Trustee to provide non-beneficiaries with a Certification of Trust instead of a full copy of the Trust document. The Certification of Trust is a document showing the relevant parts of the Trust authorizing the person to serve as Trustee. It generally shows the history of the Trust and the new tax identification number obtained for operating the Trust. It will also show the name and address of the currently acting Trustee. It indicates how assets in the Trust are to be titled and that the Trust is no longer changeable.

This is generally a two-page document and will be accepted by all major institutions, such as banks and brokerage firms, allowing the Trustee authority to access all accounts. The only exception will be real estate title companies. Title companies will want to see the portion of the Trust granting authority for the Trustee to sell or encumber real property. They generally want to make a copy of the page in the original Trust granting authority to the Trustee to convey title. See Figure 4 for an example Certification of Trust form.

6. Obtain certified death certificates.

In the State of Florida, the Bureau of Vital Statistics provides a short and a long form of death certificates. The short form is the death certificate that does not include the cause of death (and may actually be printed on a long piece of paper). The long form includes the cause of death. The Trustee should obtain both types.

7. Open safe-deposit box.

The decedent's safe-deposit box should be located and opened. Occasionally, the important estate documents will actually be located in the safe-deposit box, which would make it difficult to go forward with the Trust administration until the box is opened. But if the original Trust document is in the box, it may be difficult for the Trustee to show that he or she is the appointed successor Trustee for the Trust estate.

If the safe-deposit box is in the decedent's name only, the Trustee can fill out a Request to Open Safe-Deposit Box letter, as shown in Figure 5. When presented to the bank, the bank should allow the Trustee to open the box and remove the original Will, deed, or burial information and original insurance policies from the safe-deposit box. A bank employee will be with the Trustee recording all the box's contents and will retain copies of any original documents removed by the Trustee. All other assets in the box, including the original Trust document, must remain there until the appropriate court authorization allows the bank to release the box and its contents. The Personal Representative appointed in the Will to administer the decedent's probate estate must petition the court, through an attorney, to remove the contents.

Occasionally, the question is whether or not the decedent even has a safe-deposit box. Sometimes a family member will say they thought dad had a safe-deposit box, but there is no immediate indication there is one. Evidence of a safe-deposit box agreement or a key will indicate there is a safe-deposit box. If these items cannot be located, then the Trustee should check the decedent's checkbook register for a one-year period to see if a payment for a safe-deposit box was made. A call to the decedent's bank could answer the question, also. Otherwise, it may be necessary to write a blanket letter to all the banks in the area asking if they have a record for a safe-deposit box titled in the name of the decedent.

8. File original Pour-Over Will with clerk of the court in county where decedent lived.

In Florida, there is a statutory requirement that the original Last Will and Testament, including Pour-Over Wills, be filed with the clerk of the court in the county in which the decedent was domiciled within 10 days after receiving information the Testator is deceased (Fla. Stat. § 732.901). This means the Trustee will file the original Will with the county clerk where the decedent lived. The original document will be kept by the clerk on permanent record and never returned. That is why it is imperative to make photocopies before depositing the original. However, if a copy of the Will cannot be located once it has been filed, anyone can go to the clerk of court and purchase a certified copy.

9. Change address at the Post Office.

Once the Trustee has accepted the position and the Certification of Trust is signed, the mail should no longer be going to the decedent's residence but to the Trustee's business or residence. The Trustee should change the address using the appropriate postal forms from the local Post Office or submitting the change online at www.usps.com for a small fee.

10. File Notice of Trust.

Fla. Stat. § 736.05055 requires a Trustee assuming responsibility for the Trust to notify the court. This is done through a statutory notice called Notice of Trust. The form is not filed in the newspaper like the notice filed for a probate estate. It is simply a notice filed with the clerk of the court in the county in which the decedent was domiciled. See Figure 6 for an example Notice of Trust.

11. Review the named beneficiaries and compare them to the interested parties.

The distribution of the Trust may not be as straightforward as it first appears. Certain beneficiaries named in the Trust may not legally be entitled to claim a share or receive a gift from the Trust. It is also possible that individuals who were not named as a beneficiary will have a right to a share of the Trust. The advice of a licensed Florida attorney should be sought prior to any distribution if the Trustee has concerns about a named or omitted beneficiary. Examples of the exclusion of a named beneficiary and the inclusion of an unnamed beneficiary are provided below.

- If the Trustor's former spouse was named as a beneficiary of the Trust prior to the divorce, dissolution or annulment, and the Trust and the judgment for divorce do not provide otherwise, Fla. Stat. § 736.1105 states the provision(s) related to the spouse will become void upon annulment or entry of the judgment for dissolution or divorce. Similarly, if the former spouse was named as a beneficiary of certain assets outside of the Trust and the judgment does not provide otherwise, Fla. Stat. § 732.703 states the designation of the spouse as the beneficiary is void, and the asset will pass as if the former spouse predeceased the decedent. Assets subject to this statute may include certain life insurance policies, qualified annuities, employee benefit plans, individual retirement accounts, payable-on-death accounts, and transfer-on-death accounts and securities. A former spouse should not be able to profit from a Trustor's failure to update their estate planning documents or beneficiary designations, and these statutes ensure that does not happen.

- When estate planning documents are not reviewed and updated on a regular basis, it is quite possible intended beneficiaries will not have been included or named in the Trust. If the document was executed prior to the Trustor's valid marriage, the surviving spouse is referred to as a pretermitted spouse. If said spouse has not waived their rights, is not provided for, and there is no intent specified in the Trust to omit the spouse, they will be provided for pursuant to Florida Statute and possibly share in the estate assets. If a child is born after the execution of the Trust, they may not be a named beneficiary, but they may be entitled to a share as a pretermitted child.

The Trust document should be reviewed to see if it sets forth the definition of a child that is to be used in regard to distributions. For example, the definition may or may not include adopted children, and may or may not include stepchildren. The Trust will likely include language that requires a beneficiary to survive the Trustor by a certain amount of time in order to receive their distribution. For example, some Trusts indicate if a beneficiary dies within sixty days of the Trustor's death, they are considered to have predeceased the Trustor and their estate will not receive the share.

The Trustor may also have contractual obligations entitling an unnamed beneficiary to a share of the estate. The Trustee should review any and all contracts and court orders, including, but not limited to, prenuptial agreements, postnuptial agreements, divorce decrees, and child support orders to determine if any assets are to be set aside and distributed outside of the Trust.

12. Determine if the surviving spouse has waived their rights under Florida Statute.

A surviving spouse is required to receive certain statutory amounts and allowances from the deceased spouse's estate. If the decedent did not provide the statutory minimum, their spouse is entitled to claim certain rights. The rights may be waived, wholly or partly, by a written contract, agreement, or waiver signed by the waiving party in the presence of two subscribing witnesses. The waiver can be signed before or after marriage, and are most commonly seen in the form of prenuptial and postnuptial agreements. In the absence of a valid agreement waiving these rights, the Trustee will need to determine if the surviving spouse is going to elect to claim the statutory entitlements. The most significant rights include the elective share and the homestead property.

The spouse has a right to a 30 percent share of the elective estate of the decedent. The elective estate includes assets subject to probate and certain assets passing outside of probate, such as those payable on death to a beneficiary and those assets in a revocable Trust.

There are very strict rules regarding the devise of homestead property, if a decedent is survived by a spouse or minor children and the property is not owned as tenants by the entireties or as joint tenants with rights of survivorship. If the homestead was not devised as authorized by law and the constitution, the spouse has two options. The standard option gives the surviving spouse a life estate in the homestead property with the remainder interest vesting in the decedent's descendants. With a life estate, the surviving spouse has the right to use or occupy the real property for the remainder of their life. In lieu of a life estate, the second option allows the surviving spouse to elect to take an undivided one-half (1/2) interest in the homestead property, as a tenant in common, with the remaining undivided one-half (1/2) interest vesting in the decedent's descendants.

The paragraphs above are a brief description of two of the elections that may be exercised. Every case is different, and there are many factors that need to be considered when the surviving spouse has not received the statutory amounts. Contact a licensed Florida attorney to discuss the time limits and requirement involved.

13. Obtain new Tax Identification Numbers for any continuing Trusts, such as a Special Needs Trust or Grandchildren's Trust.

Any continuing Trusts will need to be established and new tax identification numbers obtained. For example, if a beneficiary is to receive one third of the estate, but he or she is mentally handicapped/impaired, the Trustor may have directed a Special Needs Trust be created at the Trustor's death for the beneficiary's benefit. This type of Trust will continue after the distribution of everyone else's share has been made. The current Trustee may continue as the continuing Trustee, or the Trust document may appoint a separate Trustee for this continuing Special Needs Trust. The language in the Special Needs Trust will govern how it will be administered and said Trust will be required to file an annual tax return through IRS Form 1041 for every year the Trust exists. An accountant should be consulted for the preparation and filing of these returns. An accountant should also be consulted to determine what amount of taxable distributions, if any, will be made to the beneficiary.

14. Send statutorily required beneficiary letter and make copies of all Trust documents, including all amendments, and send them by certified mail to beneficiaries.

Fla. Stat. § 736.0813 requires the Trustee keep all qualified beneficiaries of the Trust reasonably informed of the Trust and its administration. A letter should be sent within 60 days of the Trustee's acceptance, and provide the required notice to all beneficiaries about their rights as to what information they are entitled to receive and what time limits they must comply with. See Figure 7 for an example letter. It specifically informs the beneficiaries that a fiduciary lawyer-client privilege in Fla. Stat. § 90.5021 applies with respect to the Trustee and any attorney employed by the Trustee and that an action to contest the validity of the Trust is limited to six months from the date the notice was sent. The Notice of Trust, the acceptance of the Trustee and the certification of Trust can be enclosed with the letter.

Upon reasonable request, the Trustee is required to send photocopies of the original Trust document and all amendments to the qualified beneficiaries. Rather than wait for a request, it is recommended that the Trustee send the copies with the statutorily required letter. Generally speaking, it is fairly straightforward that a complete photocopy of all documents should be sent to all named beneficiaries. Under certain circumstances, the Trustee can provide information relating only to a specific beneficiary. For example, the cousin who is bequeathed $5,000 may not need to know about the Special Needs Trust set up for another beneficiary, so that information may be removed or redacted from the cousin's copy.

In order to ensure each beneficiary receives their copy, each copy should be sent by certified mail. If it is just the Trustee and his sister and they are together making copies of mom's Trust document, handing her a copy is fine. However, if the sister dies in a tragic car accident and her distrusting husband now becomes the sole beneficiary of her share, then what proof does the Trustee have showing compliance with these statutory requirements?

B. Second Stage of Trust Administration: Managing the Assets

- ☐ 1. Locate assets titled in the name of the Trust or payable to the Trust.
- ☐ 2. Make copies of all financial information.
- ☐ 3. Obtain accounting and tax records.
- ☐ 4. Review all bills.
- ☐ 5. Contact real estate appraisers for real property appraisal.
- ☐ 6. Set up accounting records and separate bank accounts.
- ☐ 7. Review insurance on all major assets, such as the house and car.
- ☐ 8. Cancel credit cards and utilities.
- ☐ 9. Leave the joint account with the decedent's name still on it for cashing small checks.
- ☐ 10. Prepare and provide Trust inventory.

1. Locate assets titled in the name of the Trust or payable to the Trust.

The Trustee will need to locate any assets titled in the name of the Trust or payable to the Trust and make sure they are identified with the new tax identification number. This can be the hard part. Hopefully, the decedent fully funded the Trust and made copies of all relevant documents and placed them with the original Trust paperwork, package or book. If that is the case, it would then be a matter of taking the original Trust document or Certification of Trust to the various banks or brokerage firms and obtaining control over the decedent's Trust assets.

Unfortunately, in most cases, the decedent has not done a great job in keeping their financial documents organized. It is incumbent upon the new Trustee to locate all relevant financial information. In fact, it is their duty to do this. Often, it requires searching through every scrap of mail at the decedent's house. The checkbook for the prior year should be reviewed for purchases of assets. The tax returns for at least three prior years should also be reviewed. The financial advisor and the estate attorney should be contacted. Some estate planning attorneys have a record of the assets of the decedent while others have no such relevant information. If an asset list was obtained 15 years ago and the client has not updated it, then it is generally of little help to the Trustee.

An account titled in the Trust name that allows the Trustee access is obviously a Trust asset. Any account the Trustee is unable to access has one or two different solutions. If the account is joint with someone else, generally the survivor on the account owns the money or asset. If the account is solely in the decedent's name, it is not immediately a Trust asset and will require a separate legal proceeding called probate in order for the asset to be retitled to the Trust and be controlled by the Trustee.

- If the Trustee is not sure if the asset is a Trust asset, hire an attorney.
- If a debt is owed to the decedent and is not being paid, hire an attorney.
- If an account is jointly titled with someone else and the Trustee thinks it should be a Trust asset, hire an attorney.
- If the Trustee needs to clear up legal title to real property, hire an attorney

2. Make copies of all financial information.

Copies of bank statements, check registers, investment accounts, CDs, property deeds, and promissory notes are all required to be given to the beneficiaries. Not only are the beneficiaries entitled to know what the decedent had at the time of death, they may also be entitled to know what happened to the assets prior to death. For example, the decedent may have been taken advantage of by a beneficiary or neighbor or financial advisor.

3. Obtain accounting and tax records.

The Trustee is personally liable for the decedent's taxes. This means if the Trustee gives away all of the decedent's money to the beneficiaries and then a tax bill comes due, the IRS will pursue the

Trustee, personally. In order to avoid this, the Trustee should take precautions to ensure all tax obligations have been paid prior to making the final distribution of estate assets.

The first step is to contact the decedent's CPA or bookkeeper to ensure the last 1040 tax return has been timely filed. A determination should be made if the decedent owed money or will be receiving a refund. The Trustee can engage the CPA to continue on and File a 1041 tax return, if the estate assets generate any income above $600 for the year. The CPA should also be consulted if the decedent died with assets greater than the estate tax exemption. Currently, that amount is $5,490,000. If the decedent had more than the exemption amount at death, Form 706 Estate (and Generation-Skipping Transfer) Tax Return would be due and tax payments might need to be made.

Occasionally, the Trustee steps into a decedent's Trust estate and has no idea about any prior tax returns or whether or not a tax return has ever been filed. If the decedent's income is low enough, there may not have been a requirement for a tax return to be filed. However, with personal liability exposure in mind, the Trustee should be very certain there are no tax obligations due and owing before beneficiary distributions are made. The IRS forms used to eliminate exposure are discussed in Stage Three.

4. Review all bills.

Just because the Trustor is dead does not mean all of the Trustor's creditors can go unpaid. All valid outstanding bills and debts of the decedent should be paid. Generally, insurance on the vehicles and home should be a first priority. Likewise, utility bills on the main house should be paid immediately. Other bills, such as credit card bills and other debts, should be thoroughly reviewed to determine if they are valid and if they should be paid. Most often, medical bills should not be paid for at least six months or more. The insurance companies generally take about six months to settle on what the final bill, if any, would be due from the decedent. Remember, we are no longer worried about the decedent's credit at this point.

5. Contact real estate appraisers for real property appraisal.

The last, greatest tax break occurs upon death. All of the decedent's assets receive a stepped-up tax basis. What the decedent paid for the land or the stock ceases to be of interest, since all that matters now is what the market value was on the date of the decedent's death. That means, when the beneficiaries sell the property, they will not have to pay capital gains taxes from the date when the decedent originally purchased the property. In essence, the capital gains taxes are forgiven. Likewise, if an apartment complex has been depreciated, it also receives a stepped-up tax basis, and the new beneficiaries will not be required to worry about capital gains taxes or depreciation recapture.

Once the appraiser has appraised the property at fair market value, that value will be the new cost basis for the property. The beneficiary will only pay capital gains tax on the difference between the appraisal amount and the sale price, if any. As a planning technique, if the estate is one not owing estate death taxes (i.e., generally an estate less than $5,490,000, or the current exemption amount), the appraisals should be on the high side. The Trustee should ask the appraiser to give a high-value within his subjective range. Assure him the appraisal will not be used for sale or mortgage purposes but to establish a new cost tax basis.

6. Set up accounting records and separate bank accounts.

The Trustee has a fiduciary duty to account for every asset in the estate. The accounting records should be kept from the very first day the Trustee assumes the position. Unless the estate is very simple and small, a bookkeeper or CPA may be needed to assist in setting up the bookkeeping records. At a minimum, keep every single receipt. Never pay cash for anything. Never use a debit card for estate purchases.

The Trustee should obtain a Trust estate checkbook and pay for all debts through that account. The Trustee should never commingle Trust estate assets with their own money. Any violation of these rules may subject the Trustee to civil as well as criminal penalties. If all the records have been properly kept from the beginning, the final accounting will be easier to complete before final distribution is made.

The Trustee should never deposit their own funds into the Trust account nor deposit Trust account funds into their personal account. The Trustee should not pay Trust bills with their personal money nor should they pay their personal account bills with Trust account money. The only exception regarding the use of personal funds to pay an estate bill might be where the Trustee assumes the Trustee position and finds the house utility bill overdue and ready for termination. It is acceptable for the Trustee to pay that utility bill out of their own funds and then reimburse themselves immediately once they have access to Trust funds.

7. Review insurance on all major assets, such as the house and car.

The Trustee is personally liable for the Trust property. This fact poses a significant liability exposure to the Trustee. The first order of business for a new Trustee should be to assure that all real property and motor vehicles are adequately insured. It is imperative that the Trustee phone the decedent's insurance agent or, if none, retain a brand new insurance agent in order to review all existing policies and/or to acquire new ones if necessary.

Some policies have a grace period that will keep the insurance effective even after the insured client dies. The insurance agent should be able to determine how long this grace period lasts. Replacement insurance should be obtained for all Trust assets before the current policies lapse. It is very likely this replacement insurance will cost more than the original policies. This is because most properties will no longer be owner occupied. They will be vacant properties owned by a Trust estate. Insurance companies tend to believe this is a higher risk than an owner occupied property and will charge more for this insurance.

This insurance is so important it must be the first priority when a Trustee takes over. If there is no estate cash available to pay for the insurance and the Trustee is a family member, it might be wise to use the Trustee's personal funds to pay for the insurance. The

Trustee could then sell the most likely asset to reimburse themselves for this expense. Of course, if the Trustee thinks they are stepping into a virtual minefield, the Trustee can decline the representation and not be personally liable.

Another asset creating liability for the estate is the decedent's automobile. Once the decedent dies, the insurance company has a grace period of several months. The Trustee should call the insurance company to determine how long this grace period lasts. The car should not be driven by any of the family members but should be stored on the property. It should be used only sparingly, if at all. Normally, Trustees are advised to move a vehicle out of the Trust estate as soon as possible. This can be done by either giving the vehicle to one of the beneficiaries as part of their share or by selling it to a third party and depositing the proceeds to a Trust account.

8. Cancel credit cards and utilities.

Once gone, the decedent's credit cards should be cut up and no longer used. It is considered fraudulent activity to continue using a decedent's credit cards. The credit card company should be notified of death, and the accounts should be closed, so that interest will no longer accrue on the account. The Trustee should review the final bill to determine what charges are valid and should be paid. This type of account should not be paid until all other assets have been located and other critical debts paid. After all other debts have been paid and there are sufficient assets in the estate, the Trustee should pay any valid credit card debt.

9. Leave the joint account with the decedent's name still on it for cashing small checks.

If the Trustee or a beneficiary happens to be a joint owner with the decedent on an account outside the Trust, that account should be left intact with the decedent's name still on it. After death, there are generally small checks that make their way back to the Trustee. One might be a return of a utility deposit, another might be the return of some insurance premium paid by the decedent. Generally, the Trustee will not be able to cash these checks, because there is no account still active with the decedent's individual name still on it. If the joint account is left active, the Trustee can simply write "for deposit only" on the back of the check payable to the decedent, and the bank will most often accept the check and deposit it into the joint account. Otherwise, the small amounts may simply be forfeited, because the cost of opening a probate to cash the checks will be far more than the value of the checks.

10. Prepare and provide Trust inventory.

Fla. Stat. § 736.0813(1)(e) says upon reasonable request, the Trustee shall provide a qualified beneficiary with relevant information about the assets and liabilities of the Trust and the particulars relating to administration. Rather than wait for a request, it is recommended that the Trustee prepare a Trust inventory and provide it to the beneficiaries within 60 days of assuming the Trustee position. The Trust inventory can simply be a list of all Trust assets and the approximate values. (See Figure 8 for an example Trust inventory form.)

If it is critical, the Trustee may need to get an appraisal for each parcel of real property before submitting this inventory. Most often, family members will not require this detailed inventory. They simply want photocopies of bank statements and brokerage statements, and they can determine the value of land by looking up the parcel on the official property records or real property appraiser's records.

C. Third Stage of Trust Administration: County Filings, Tax Documents and Probate

☐ 1. Review final 1040 for the decedent.
☐ 2. Determine if a Form 706, United States Estate (and Generation-Skipping Transfer) Tax Return, is required.
☐ 3. Record short death certificate form in each county where land is located.
☐ 4. Prepare the Affidavit of No Florida Estate Tax Due.
☐ 5. Prepare Affidavit of Continuous Marriage.
☐ 6. Send IRS Form 56, Notice Concerning Fiduciary Relationship, to show the Trustee is in charge of the decedent's estate.
☐ 7. Request IRS review the estate for tax liability with IRS Form 4810.
☐ 8. Request IRS release the Trustee from any personal liability with IRS Form 5495.
☐ 9. Determine if probate is needed to clear title to assets or to initiate the 90-day statute of limitations.
☐ 10. Determine if additional legal proceedings are needed for an asset

1. Review final 1040 for the decedent.

Since the Trustee is personally liable for the decedent's taxes, it would be wise to review the last year's 1040 tax return, as well as the 1040 tax return due in the year of the decedent's death. A bookkeeper or CPA should prepare this return. Occasionally, the son or daughter who is acting as the Trustee has been doing mom or dad's taxes for years. In that case, they most likely will not be concerned with tax issues.

2. Determine if a Form 706, United States Estate (and Generation-Skipping Transfer) Tax Return, is required.

If the estate assets do not exceed $5,490,000 (or the current exemption amount), then an estate tax return, IRS Form 706, will not be required. However, if the gross assets of the estate exceed this credit amount, even though the net assets will fall far below that amount, the return is still due. As an example, if the land is worth $6,000,000 but has an outstanding mortgage of $4,000,000, the net estate is only $2,000,000. Clearly, no estate taxes will be due, but the Form 706 tax return will still need to be completed and filed. All Form 706 tax returns must be filed with the IRS within nine months from the date of the decedent's death. A one-time, automatic six-month extension can be granted. However, any taxes will be required to be paid on the original nine month due date, and not on the six month extension date.

Even if estate taxes are not due, a Form 706 tax return may still be filed to preserve the first spouse's credit amount. Under the tax law, the first spouse to die has an unused tax credit that is portable to the surviving spouse. However, the only way to make this unused exemption portable is to file a Form 706 tax return immediately after the death of the first spouse. This tax return normally requires a seasoned tax professional, so unless the Trustee is such a professional, a law firm or certified public accountant should be hired to make sure this portability election is properly preserved.

3. Record short death certificate form in each county where land is located.

The Trustee will need to have a short form death certificate recorded in each county where land is located. (County clerks will only accept the short form death certificate with no cause of death listed.) Once the short form death certificate has been recorded in the county official records, the original document will be returned. If the decedent died outside of Florida and the Trustee is only able to obtain a certificate with the cause of death, the Florida county clerk will accept the form and redact the cause of death from the official record.

4. Prepare the Affidavit of No Florida Estate Tax Due.

This is a form provided by the State of Florida that shows the estate does not require the filing of a federal estate and gift tax return, Form 706. Generally, if the estate is less than

$5,490,000 (or the current exemption amount), then this form should be signed and recorded in each county where the decedent owned real property. If the estate is one where it exceeds this amount or there is a requirement for a federal tax return to be filed (706), this form should not be signed and sent. An example form is in Figure 9.

5. Prepare Affidavit of Continuous Marriage.

If the Trustor was married at the time of death and owned a homestead property or other real property with their spouse as tenants by the entireties (husband and wife), the Trustee should complete an Affidavit of Continuous Marriage form. It will typically state the date the couple were married, that they remained married until the death of the Trustor, and the particulars of the real property. The purpose of the affidavit is to clear title to the surviving spouse by providing proof the tenancy by the entireties was valid at the time of the Trustor's death. By doing this, any liens that may have attached, if filed against the individual Trustor, will be defeated. The affidavit is not required by statute but will typically be required by a title company in any future property transaction. See Figure 10 for an example of the affidavit.

6. Send IRS Form 56, Notice Concerning Fiduciary Relationship, to show the Trustee is in charge of the decedent's estate.

The Trustee should submit IRS Form 56, Notice Concerning Fiduciary Relationship, to the IRS to let them know that the Trustee has assumed this special fiduciary relationship on behalf of the decedent's estate. All correspondence will then be made directly through the Trustee to the IRS, and the IRS will make all correspondence back for the Trust estate to the Trustee. As explained in Stage 4, once the estate is complete, the Trustee will send another copy of IRS Form 56, completing the Termination section, to announce that the Trustee is ceasing their duties, responsibilities and obligations for the Trust estate. See Figure 11 for a copy of Form 56, Notice Concerning Fiduciary Relationship.

7. Request IRS review the estate for tax liability with IRS Form 4810.

The Trustee should use IRS Form 4810 to request that the IRS review the decedent's last three years of tax returns. The completed tax returns should be attached to the form. See Figure 12 for a copy of Form 4810. If the IRS identifies any tax liability, it will be the Trustee's responsibility to satisfy the debt.

8. Request IRS release the Trustee from any personal liability with IRS Form 5495.

Once the IRS has finished the review requested in the previous step, and the Trustee has paid any tax liability, the Trustee should submit IRS Form 5495, which requests the IRS to discharge the Trustee from personal liability. See Figure 13 for a copy of Form 5495.

9. Determine if probate is needed to clear title to assets or to initiate the 90-day statute of limitations.

Any assets that cannot be controlled by the Trustee and are not payable or transferable to a named beneficiary will require probate. Probate is a court-supervised process for defining and gathering the assets of a deceased person. A petition is filed with the court, and the court supervises and appoints a Personal Representative to stand in the shoes of the decedent, so all debts are identified and paid, and eventually the remaining assets will be distributed to the decedent's Trust beneficiaries. Probate costs money because it involves attorneys, Personal Representatives, and court supervision. The cost of probate is generally around 4% to 8% of the estate value going through probate.

Probate also involves a time element. The average probate in the United States runs around 13 months. Even with an efficient probate firm, a simplified estate, and compliant heirs, the time frame for a formal probate in Florida is between six months and one year. Probate is a public process where an original Will is filed with the clerk and becomes public record. For one dollar a page, anyone can get a copy of a Will and determine what the decedent wanted done with the estate assets and who was in and who was out.

A Trust, on the other hand, is a private document and is never recorded in the public records of Florida. Typically, an individual with a Living Revocable Trust has a Pour-Over Will as part of their estate planning. This Will names the Trust as the sole beneficiary of any probate estate, so it essentially "pours" the probate asset back into the Trust. Once the asset is retitled to the Trust through the probate process, the Trustee will manage and distribute the asset pursuant to the terms of the Trust.

Any assets such as land or a promissory note located outside of Florida will require a separate probate. This is referred to as an ancillary probate and is supplemental to the probate conducted in Florida. The proceeding will require separate lawyers licensed to practice in the other state and will be an additional expense of the estate. A parcel of land from another state titled in the Trust will avoid probate in the State of Florida, as well as the other state where the land is located.

Probate may also be used to shorten the time period in which the Trustee and beneficiaries remain liable to creditors of the decedent. Florida has a two-year statute of limitations for any outstanding creditor claims. If nothing is done and two years has passed since the decedent died, any debt or claim is extinguished by law. The creditor cannot pursue their debt, if they have not made arrangements to pursue it before that time. The administration of the Trust requires no formal notice be sent to creditors. A Trustee is under an obligation to pay all appropriate debts of the decedent. However, a creditor may initiate a probate and request the Trustee pay the decedent's debt. If the Trustee has already made distributions, this could be a problem for both the Trustee and the beneficiaries. The Trustee will have no money to defend themself, and the beneficiaries may be dragged into litigation after they have already spent their inheritance. Out of an abundance of caution, occasionally a Trustee will initiate a probate proceeding to place a notice in the newspaper that shortens this timeframe from two years to 90 days. The majority of corporate Trust departments file this separate probate to shorten that timeframe even though there are no assets passing through the probate estate. This precautionary probate is not needed for most families; however, it is available for the Trustee who wants to eliminate any possibility of a problem down the road.

10. Determine if additional legal proceedings are needed for an asset.

In some cases, additional legal proceedings may be necessary in order to obtain proper title to an asset. Some proceedings may have been initiated during the life of the decedent and will have to be continued by his or her Personal Representative. Some issues may be created after the person's death, and a new proceeding will have to be started by the decedent's representative.

If a debt is owed to the decedent and it is not being paid, the Trustee is responsible for collection. Some people may incorrectly believe that the debt was erased by the death, but a certified letter explaining the terms of the repayment is often sufficient to get the payments back on track. If the payee fails to respond or make a payment, a lawsuit may be the only remedy.

Under Florida law, if an account is jointly titled with someone else, it is presumed the owner intended the property to pass to the surviving party, rather than to the deceased person's heirs as identified in the Trust. The presumption may be overcome only by proof of fraud, or undue influence, or clear and convincing proof of a contrary intent. For example, if the decedent added the joint owner to act as an agent on his or her behalf and there was no intent for the joint owner to inherit the "convenience account," it will belong to the decedent's estate. If the joint owner believes he or she is entitled to the funds, litigation may be necessary in order to prove the intent of the decedent and contradict the presumption.

If there is an issue with real property, such as a cloud on the title or a dispute over ownership or property lines, a legal proceeding may be necessary to clear legal title for the Trust. The use of an incomplete legal description, the use of an incomplete or incorrect Trust name, the failure of all owners to sign the deed, and the failure of a divorce decree to properly transfer ownership to one spouse are just a few examples of property issues that may be discovered after the decedent's death.

If any of these situations are present, the Trustee must seek the advice of a Florida attorney.

D. Fourth Stage of Trust Administration: Final Accounting and Distribution

- ☐ 1. Distribute personal and household items.
- ☐ 2. Obtain updated asset valuation for distribution.
- ☐ 3. Obtain updated liability information for distribution.
- ☐ 4. Prepare proposed plan of distribution and consider partial distribution.
- ☐ 5. Prepare annual Trust accounting or obtain Trust accounting waivers from beneficiaries.
- ☐ 6. Prepare final accounting with plan for distribution and Final Waiver, Receipt, Release and Refunding Agreement.
- ☐ 7. Have attorney prepare transfer documents, such as deeds, assignments of interest, and new stock certificates for family held businesses.
- ☐ 8. Distribute assets to the beneficiaries.
- ☐ 9. Send IRS Form 56 to terminate the Trustee's fiduciary relationship.

1. Distribute personal and household items.

Distribute personal items to family members in any manner convenient and agreed upon. Flip a coin, draw straws or pick numbers to determine who goes first and then pick in the order agreed to until all desired items have been selected. The remaining items can be sold at an estate sale or given to a charity.

2. Obtain updated asset valuation for distribution.

Prior to final distribution of the Trust estate, the assets should be revalued unless an agreement has been made otherwise. A number of factors could have caused the value to go up or down in the time since the decedent passed away. If the Trustee is dividing the estate between two beneficiaries, the heirs want to be assured they are each receiving exactly 50%. If one particular asset passes to one beneficiary as part of his share and this asset has dramatically increased in value, an unfair and unequal distribution would be the result. Unless otherwise stated in the document, the assets are valued at the time of distribution to determine their final values so the shares can be properly divided.

3. Obtain updated liability information for distribution.

Prior to final distribution, the Trustee will want to ensure all debts and liabilities have been eliminated. If a creditor comes forward after the final distribution has been made, the Trustee will have no funds to pay the creditor or fight the creditor claim. More importantly, the Trustee may be responsible for the debt.

4. Prepare proposed plan of distribution and consider partial distribution.

Prepare a distribution schedule. This will show the Trustee's proposed distribution, who gets what, and so forth. A preliminary schedule like this can be passed around to the beneficiaries, so there are no surprises when the final distribution is made. See an example form in Figure 14. The form includes language that will invoke the six-month limitation period pursuant to Fla. Stat. § 736.1008(4)(c). This provision specifically advises the beneficiary that an action against the Trustee for breach of Trust is barred for any beneficiary who has received this information unless the action or claim is started within six months after the receipt of this notice.

There is no requirement that all Trust estate assets must be held until final distribution. Partial distributions can be made at the Trustee's discretion and outlined on a proposed plan of distribution. Under most normal family scenarios, a parent dies and the children all get along. Most of the bills have been paid, and there are no tax obligations. It is appropriate for the Trustee to make partial distributions of estate assets rather than holding them all until the end. A partial distribution can be a $5,000, $10,000, or even $100,000 payment.

When a partial distribution is going to be made in cash or in kind, (such as with land or stock), the beneficiary should sign a Partial Receipt and Release Agreement acknowledging that he or she received that portion as a partial distribution from their share of the Trust estate. See Figure 15 for an example Partial Receipt and Release Agreement.

The steps a Trustee should take if a beneficiary objects to the proposed plan of distribution or if they refuse to sign a Partial Receipt and Release Agreement are outlined on pages 39 and 40 of Section E, Problems.

5. Prepare annual Trust accounting or obtain Trust accounting waivers from beneficiaries.

Pursuant to Fla. Stat. § 736.0813(1)(d), the Trustee is required to provide a Trust accounting from the date of the last accounting or, if none, from the date on which the Trustee became accountable to each qualified beneficiary at least annually.

Fla. Stat. § 736.0813(2) provides that qualified beneficiaries can sign a Waiver of Annual/Final Accounting to notify the Trustee that the accounting will not be required. For some families, the Trustee simply gives a list of all the assets to the family members, and they sign a waiver, so no formal accounting is required. An example of the Waiver form can be found in Figure 16. However, if the waiver is not signed by all beneficiaries, the Trustee MUST prepare the annual/final accounting.

An example form for the Trust accounting is provided in Figure 17. Generally, the accounting must be in a reasonably understandable format and must contain a statement identifying the Trust, the name of the Trustee, and the time period covered by the accounting.

The form requires the Trustee begin by determining a starting balance. This means the Trustee will identify the appropriate date of death value of the assets taken into the Trust or use the amount from the close of the last accounting period. Once this starting balance is obtained, the accounting form contains a schedule for payments received by the Trust, such as insurance policy proceeds and utility refunds. The second schedule is for the disbursements, meaning expenses of the Trust estate. The third schedule details all distributions paid to the beneficiaries from estate assets. The fourth schedule allows for capital transactions to be identified. For example, property appraised at the date of death for $100,000 may now have a new value of $200,000 because of appreciation. Conversely, property valued on the date of death for $100,000 may have a $50,000 value at the time of distribution, because the property was found to be contaminated. This schedule allows for those gains or losses to be adjusted. Finally, the last schedule on the accounting form outlines the assets on hand including any additional new assets discovered. The letter that accompanies the accounting includes the six-month limitation period language discussed previously.

If the Trustee believes that no beneficiary will object to the accounting, they can reduce the six-month period by providing a separate form to each beneficiary that acknowledges they have received and reviewed the annual/final accounting, they have no objection to the accounting and they release the Trustee from liability associated with the accounting. If this form is signed by all beneficiaries, the Trustee can proceed immediately with the knowledge that an objection will not be filed. An example of the No Objection to Annual/Final Accounting form can be found in Figure 18.

If, on the other hand, a beneficiary objects to the accounting, the Trustee has no option but to hire a lawyer and follow the steps outlined on page 40 of Section E, Problems.

6. Prepare final accounting with plan for distribution and Final Waiver, Receipt, Release and Refunding Agreement.

Fla. Stat. § 736.0813(1)(d) also requires the Trustee provide a Trust accounting on termination of the Trust or on change of the Trustee, unless waived by the beneficiaries (see above). The same format provided for the annual accounting above can be used for the final accounting as well. Additionally, Fla. Stat. § 736.08135(2)(f) requires the Trustee include a plan of distribution for any undistributed assets shown on the final accounting with the report. This can be done in the same format as the proposed plan of distribution outlined above. If all the beneficiaries have waived their right to a final accounting, the Trustee should provide each beneficiary with a plan for distribution only.

When a distribution is going to be made in cash or in kind, (such as with land or stock), the beneficiary should sign a Final Waiver, Receipt, Release and Refunding Agreement. (An example of this form is provided in Figure 19.) In it, the beneficiary acknowledges he or she received the identified asset(s) as final distribution of their share, relieves the Trustee of any further responsibility or liability related to the asset received, and relieves the Trustee of any further liability or accounting responsibilities as related to the Trust.

If a beneficiary objects to the final accounting, objects to the plan of distribution or if they refuse to sign a Final Waiver, Receipt, Release and Refunding Agreement, the Trustee should refer to pages 39 and 40 of Section E, Problems, for the appropriate responses.

7. Have attorney prepare transfer documents, such as deeds, assignments of interest, and new stock certificates for family held businesses.

Once final distributions have been decided upon, usually an attorney will prepare transfer documents such as deeds, assignments of interest and new stock certificates for closely held family businesses. The Trustee will then sign all such documents, and the attorney will generally record them in the appropriate official records. A special deed called a Trustee's deed will be used to transfer real estate owned by the Trust out of the Trust to the intended beneficiary. If the property is being sold to an unrelated buyer, then, generally, a title company will prepare these transfer documents.

8. Distribute assets to the beneficiaries.

Once the Trustee has received a signed Final Waiver, Receipt, Release and Refunding Agreement from each beneficiary, they can make final distributions. It is recommended that all distributions be sent using a trackable delivery method that requires a signature upon delivery. Any funds that are not sent electronically should be transferred by check so there is a financial record of the funds being deposited.

9. Send IRS Form 56 to terminate the Trustee's fiduciary relationship.

At the beginning of the administrative process, the Trustee submitted IRS Form 56, Notice Concerning Fiduciary Relationship, in order to inform the IRS that the Trustee was assuming this special fiduciary relationship on behalf of the decedent's estate. At this point, the Trustee should use the same form in order to inform them this relationship has terminated. See Figure 11 for Form 56.

E. Problems

There are so many potential problems that can arise during this process that no guide can cover them all. However, this section will give you some guidance for dealing with the more common issues that arise when administering a Trust. If the Trustee experiences any of these problems or a serious issue not discussed in this section, they must seek advice from a licensed Florida attorney.

1. Trustee wants to decline or resign

The fact a person is appointed to serve as successor Trustee, does not create an obligation for them to do so. If the appointee has not accepted the appointment as successor Trustee, has not accepted any assets for administration and has not performed an act of administration of or related to the Trust, they can decline the position. Unless the terms of the Trust outline a specific method of declination, the appointee will typically send a written statement declining the position to either their successor named in the Trust, or if no one is named, to the qualified beneficiaries of the Trust.

If a person has accepted the appointment of successor Trustee but no longer wishes to serve, they can resign from the position. Again, unless the terms of the Trust outline a specific method of resignation, the Trustee will send a written statement resigning to their successor or the qualified beneficiaries. A resigning Trustee will most likely have to do an accounting before the resignation is finalized.

If the declination or resignation of the Trustee creates a vacancy in trusteeship with no other Trustee remaining, Fla. Stat. § 736.0704 outlines the order in which the vacancy shall be filled: 1) by a person named pursuant to the terms of the Trust, 2) by a person appointed by unanimous agreement of the qualified beneficiaries or 3) by court appointment.

2. Tax problems

a. Unpaid 1040 IRS Taxes

Occasionally, the son or daughter who lives in town has been preparing or assisting in the preparation of the decedent's tax return for the last several years. They have either done the returns themselves or dealt directly with the CPA. They know the taxes have been paid, and there are no outstanding liabilities of any kind. For the rest of us, it may not be that straightforward. The Trustee shows up at the decedent's house a day after his or her death; they open the door, look inside, and find it is a mess. There are piles and piles of unopened envelopes. Now it dawns on the Trustee that the decedent's mental condition has been declining for years, and they may not have been taking care of financial business. An early indicator is a huge pile of unopened envelopes. The Trustee's duty is to organize the envelopes and sort through any containing financial information, whether it be assets or debts.

Once the financial information has been properly sorted through, the decedent's CPA should be contacted. If they do not have a CPA, then the Trustee should hire one. The Trustee should review the tax returns for the last three years. Occasionally, the decedent will not have filed taxes for the last three years. This may be due to neglect on their part or because their income was so low they were not required to file a return. All this paperwork should be given to the CPA, and the CPA should make the final decision as to whether or not a tax return should be filed and what, if any, taxes should be paid. Occasionally, the CPA will say a refund is due, and a return will be filed to obtain that refund. The Trustee has an absolute duty to ensure these tax issues are resolved.

Once the CPA has all the proper information, the tax return will be filed at the normal time in April the following year. If the decedent is entitled to a refund, a complete distribution of estate assets can be made prior to this time. If taxes are due, the Trustee should simply retain enough money to pay the taxes and the final CPA fees, and the remaining amount can be distributed to the beneficiaries. The Trustee is entitled to keep a reserve for this purpose.

b. Estate tax – Form 706

If the gross estate, that means the value of all assets owned in the Trust estate, add up to more than $5,490,000 (or the current exemption amount), then Form 706, United States Estate (and Generation-Skipping Transfer) Tax Return must be filed. The tax return is approximately 52 pages in length and requires the services of a knowledgeable CPA. Even if the estate will owe no taxes, sometimes the return may still be required. This is so, even if the net amount of the estate is far less than the exemption amount. For example, if the real property in the estate has a value of $6 million with an outstanding mortgage of $4 million, the estate will have a net value of only $2 million. No taxes will be due, but the Form 706 tax return is still required to be filed because the gross estate exceeds the exemption amount.

Any net asset above the exempt amount is taxed at the rate of 40%. That means every dollar above the current exemption amount of $5,490,000 will be taxed at 40 cents on the dollar. It is imperative the Trustee engage competent legal counsel and tax assistance in order to make sure the taxes are properly and timely paid. Also, there are ways to lower the estate value for IRS tax consideration. Consult with an estate planning lawyer for ways to accomplish this goal.

The Form 706 tax return is due within nine months of death. There is a one-time six-month extension. However, any taxes that may be due must be paid within the original nine-month timeframe, and not during the six-month extension.

c. Trust tax – 1041, Fiduciary Tax Return

Once the Trustee has accepted the job and a new tax identification number has been obtained for the Trust assets, any income generated from those assets must be reported to the IRS. This report is done on a 1041 tax return. This is also called a Fiduciary Tax return. It is not the Trustee's money or income, but they are required to properly account for it and ensure the IRS receives the taxes on any income. The Trustee will be held personally responsible for unpaid taxes or errors.

d. Heirs with tax lien issues

This is a thorny issue that must be resolved pretty much on a case-by-case basis. Most estate lawyers want to know from the client if a beneficiary has a tax lien. If known, then protective measures can be made in the Trust document to ensure the beneficiary with the tax lien does not have his or her entire inheritance taken by the IRS. However, most often, the Trustee is simply faced with an issue where Trust assets are required to be distributed, and one of the beneficiaries has an IRS tax lien. Even if the Trustee knows there is a tax lien, they are not required to notify the IRS. The only time they are required to distribute money to the IRS is if the IRS placed a lien on the estate assets.

If the Trustee administers the Trust estate according to the statutes and makes a standard distribution to the beneficiary, they should have no responsibility. However, as always, it is best to consult with an estate attorney or a certified public accountant regarding the proper procedure for distribution. The last thing the Trustee wants is an IRS problem.

If the IRS tax lien attaches to property, the property cannot be sold until the tax lien has been resolved. If there are four beneficiaries inheriting a piece of property and one has a tax lien, the IRS will encumber that one-fourth share of the property. The other three beneficiaries will not have their shares encumbered by the tax lien, but the practical effect is that the land cannot be sold unless the IRS authorizes the sale. Once sold, the IRS gets their money first, and the other beneficiaries each receive their respective shares.

3. Beneficiary problems

a. Uncooperative beneficiaries

Imagine the Trustee is the son of the decedent and his brother hates him. The brother thinks his Trustee brother talked mom into making him the Trustee. He is unhappy with what the Trustee brother is receiving from the estate, and with the fact he is receiving a Trustee's fee. The brother has stated he will not help or cooperate in any manner. The best course of action is to follow the Trustee formula. The Trustee should provide the brother with all the statutory notices, and all the statutory information and timelines for him to follow. All correspondence should be sent to him by certified mail. If this is all done properly, and the Trustee has given him all the accounting information and a plan for distribution, and he does not formally object within the statutory time limits, the Trustee simply sends him his check and is not concerned with what he says after that point.

If the brother does object, it is a simple matter to request a hearing before a judge to approve the Trustee's plan. This is a legal proceeding, and the Trustee will need to hire a lawyer. The brother can complain, but unless he has something legitimate to complain about, the judge will simply dismiss him and allow the Trustee to go forward and close the Trust estate. Normally, when closing a Trust estate, the Trustee will want to receive beneficiary receipts, releases, and waivers of accountings. If a beneficiary is uncooperative, the Trustee will have to go the route of providing a formal accounting and plan for distribution, and wait the appropriate time. Generally, once the formal accounting has been provided to the beneficiary along with the plan of distribution, then after six months have passed, they will have waived their right to contest. See Fla. Stat. § 736.1008(2) for more information on the limitations on proceedings against Trustees.

b. Minor age beneficiaries

In Florida, any child under the age of 18 is considered a minor. That means they do not have the same legal rights as an adult. Specifically, pursuant to Fla. Stat. § 710.107(3)(c), in absence of a Will or the absence of authority under a Will or Trust, minors are not able to receive assets greater than $10,000 without court approval. For minor children, a court procedure called Guardianship will be initiated, so a court appointed guardian can take possession of the minor child's money. This is an expensive and time-consuming procedure, which only delays the minor child getting the money until age 18.

Most Trusts created by Florida lawyers have a provision regarding minor beneficiaries in their Trust documents. These provisions allow the Trustee to monitor and control the money and use it for the minor beneficiary's best interest. It prevents the Trustee from being required to turn over the entire lump sum when the child reaches the age of 18 years. Some Trusts have the age of 21, some 25, some even older than that. Because most of the Trusts have language built-in for minor beneficiaries, these Trusts can continue past the time everyone else receives their distributions and avoid the expensive court supervised guardianship.

For example, there are three beneficiaries to mom's Trust, and one is a minor grandchild. When the Trust is fully administered, the two adult beneficiaries can each receive their share outright, and the minor beneficiary's one-third share will be held in a continuing

Trust. The Trust is administered with the new tax identification number until the minor beneficiary reaches the predetermined age set forth in the Trust. The Trustee of the Trust will continue administering this one-third share as an ongoing irrevocable Trust. There will be a 1041 tax return due each year, and the Trustee will be guided by the language in the Trust when it comes to making monthly or yearly distributions. Generally, the language says the Trustee has vast discretion to provide money for the minor beneficiary's needs related to health, education, and any other need determined appropriate by the Trustee. The Trustee can pay for school, college and post-graduate, buy the beneficiary a car, or even give money to the beneficiary for a down payment on a house. However, the Trustee must review the Trust document for specific instructions. A CPA should set up proper bookkeeping and make sure the yearly 1041 tax returns are timely filed, and the appropriate income taxes are paid by either the Trust or the beneficiary.

Warning: the Trustee must keep accurate records. The Trustee will be required to file an annual accounting. The accounting will go to the guardian/custodian for the minor and, once the minor attains the age of 18 years, directly to the minor. Once the minor reaches the age indicated in the Trust, a final accounting will be due showing what the minor started with and what is in the account at that time. Hopefully, if annual accountings have been done, the Trustee will simply be required to prepare the final accounting, which in essence, would be the last annual accounting due. The Trustee will not be required to go back and account for everything that has happened over the years the Trust has been in existence, if these proper annual accountings are provided.

c. Incapacitated or incompetent beneficiaries

Sometimes, the Trustee is faced with a beneficiary who is incapacitated and unable to handle financial matters or who is incompetent and, likewise, unable to handle any financial matters. Usually, the Trust will have certain definitions that will identify these conditions. Generally, most Trusts will simply allow the Trustee to continue managing the incompetent beneficiary's funds for life. The Trustee will have other options as set forth in the Trust document that might allow the Trustee to give the money to a guardian or set up a continuing Trust for the benefit of the beneficiary with alternate Trustees named. The Trustee may also be able to purchase a financial instrument to provide a lifetime monthly income for the benefit of the beneficiary. If the maker of the Trust is aware of an incompetent beneficiary, generally special terms are added to the Trust document to provide for this special beneficiary. For example, if the beneficiary is receiving or might likely receive public benefits, a Special Needs Trust might be appropriate. This Special Needs Trust as further defined below, would allow the Trustee to continue managing the beneficiary's funds but not make the beneficiary ineligible for any public support the beneficiary is currently receiving.

d. Missing beneficiaries

Occasionally, one of the named beneficiaries of the Trust cannot be located. The Trustee is required to use their best efforts to locate any missing beneficiaries. The Trustee should hire a private detective agency or missing heir search firm to locate the missing beneficiary and document the efforts made. The expense of the search is traditionally an estate expense to be shared by all beneficiaries. However, under certain circumstances, the maker of the Trust may not know where that beneficiary is and may request a search be done, with any expense for the search taken out of the missing beneficiary's share.

Most Trustees incorrectly think they will get that beneficiary's share or simply redistribute it among the remaining beneficiaries. If a diligent search has been done using all the appropriate resources available and the missing beneficiary still cannot be located, the missing beneficiary's share should be deposited into the court registry. If the missing beneficiary is later identified, they can petition the court for recovery of the money. After a certain length of time, that money will escheat to the State of Florida.

4. Beneficiary refuses to sign Partial Receipt and Release Agreement or Final Waiver, Receipt, Release and Refunding Agreement

If a beneficiary does not sign a Partial Receipt and Release Agreement or Final Waiver, Receipt, Release and Refunding

Agreement, the Trustee will invoke the six-month limitation period included on the plan for distribution. If no objection is made within six months, the Trustee is protected by the statute and can make distributions according to the plan of distribution provided to the beneficiaries. If an objection is received, the Trustee has no option but to hire a lawyer and petition the court to review the final accounting and/or distribution as previously discussed.

5. Beneficiary objects to a plan of distribution or an accounting

If a beneficiary objects to the accounting and/or the plan of distribution, the Trustee has no option but to hire a lawyer and petition the court for help and have the documents reviewed. At that hearing, the Trustee should be represented by legal counsel. During the hearing, the accounting or plan will be reviewed, probably line by line. The beneficiary will have an opportunity to examine the accounting or plan, ask questions, and make their argument to the judge that the Trustee has not done an appropriate job. The judge will ultimately decide the outcome. The judge's opinion will govern how distributions are made. If the Trustee does not agree with the judge, an appeal can be made, but this is a very time-consuming and expensive process. **Any problem regarding final distribution with a beneficiary will most likely require the Trustee to engage the services of a probate or Trust attorney to assist them**.

6. Trust contest

a. How it happens.

A Trust contest, like a Will contest, occurs when a beneficiary anticipating an inheritance is left out. The maker of a Trust, like the maker of a Will, can leave their money anywhere they choose. They can leave it to whomever, and they do not have to leave it to their family members. They can leave unequal amounts. It is their money and they can do with it as they wish, provided they have the appropriate mental capacity. A typical scenario would be where mom has three sons and one son has not seen mom for 10 or 15 years until he gets out of prison. He has nowhere to go and moves into mom's house. Six months later, the black sheep son takes mom to a local lawyer and has mom's Trust changed. The new terms give all of mom's assets to this black sheep son and leave out the other two good sons. This is done six months before mom passes away and while she was suffering from some mental issues related to Alzheimer's or dementia. The two good sons then hire a lawyer to contest the Trust document as written, since it gives the entire estate to the one black sheep son.

b. Legal elements that must be present

The standard for creating a valid Will or Trust is quite low and is referred to as testamentary capacity. The Trust maker must understand the nature of their assets. They do not have to know the exact dollar amount in the bank; they just have to know they have a checking account, a savings account, and that they own their home. Next, the maker must understand their family connections. They know they have three sons and six grandchildren and brothers and sisters and nieces and nephews. They do not have to know each relative's name, just generally know they have these family relationships. Lastly, the maker must understand the legal documents they are about to sign will transfer their assets to the individuals named in the document upon their death. If they understand these basic fundamental principles in a general way, they can create a valid Will or Trust. The standard is quite low, so even people with stage four Alzheimer's or serious dementia problems or those on their deathbed can still create a valid Will or Trust if done during a lucid moment.

The Will or Trust document itself must also be executed pursuant to Fla. Stat. § 732.502 in order to be legally valid. Generally, the Trust maker must sign at the end of the document in the presence of at least two attesting witnesses and the attesting witnesses must sign the document in the presence of the Trust maker and each other. A Will or Trust document will be considered self-proved and require no further action to validate the document, if it is acknowledged by the maker and witnesses before an officer authorized to administer oaths, such as a notary public (Fla. Stat § 732.503). Any amendment or restatement of the Trust must be executed in the same manner. A Will or Trust document is considered valid in Florida, if it complies with the laws of the jurisdiction it was executed in or the laws of the jurisdiction the maker lived in at the time it was created. **If there is a question concerning the validity of the document, seek legal counsel.**

c. As a practical matter what can an omitted beneficiary do?

If the good sons have been left out, they will need to hire an attorney to pursue their rights. Once aware something suspicious is going on, they should hire an attorney immediately. There are very critical time limits involved in estate matters, and, unless they preserve their rights, they may waive them unknowingly. If they are served formal notice, they may only have a 20-day window to file a Will contest or Trust contest.

In order for a Will or Trust contest to be successful, there must be certain elements present. The first possible element is to prove the Trust maker did not have testamentary capacity at the time the document was signed. This is a very, very, difficult thing to do, and most Will and Trust contests never actually succeed on this element.

The second element would be to prove the Trust maker was a victim of fraud, duress, mistake, or undue influence. If they were unduly influenced by an outside party, the Trust maker was not exercising their own free will. This is where most Will and Trust contest cases are won. Pursuant to Fla. Stat § 736.0406, if the creation, amendment, or restatement of a Trust is procured by fraud, duress, mistake, or undue influence, the Trust or any part so procured is void.

Mom was suffering from Alzheimer's, was in a diminished mental state, and was easily influenced. Her primary physician says this, her friends and neighbors say this, and other family members say this. The black sheep son swoops into town and is with mom 24 hours a day, essentially browbeating her into changing her estate plan and leaving everything to him. He selects the lawyer, takes mom to the lawyer's office, and then holds onto the Trust book after mom has signed it. Under this fact pattern, it would be fairly easy to show mom was unduly influenced by this black sheep son and the court would likely set aside this last change. In such a case, the court would then go back to a prior Will or Trust, where it was divided in three separate shares. The good sons can petition the court to deduct all expenses related to the contest from the black sheep son's share of the estate.

A Trust contest is very expensive and very time consuming. Doctors, friends, family and neighbors will all be deposed. Everyone will issue their opinion as to mom's mental capacity at the time the new document was signed. Usually a contest case such as this will last between one and two years, or longer.

7. Fiduciary duty and breach

   a. What can a beneficiary do?

If the Trustee of a Trust has been using Trust funds as their own personal piggy bank, the beneficiaries have many remedies. If the Trustee is not honoring the provisions of the Trust and is trying to control the Trust then they have remedies. If the Trustee is not distributing the funds in a timely fashion, then they have remedies. All of these remedies will require the help of a Florida lawyer. Once the lawyer is retained, he or she will notify the Trustee of their breaches, and hopefully the Trustee will remedy the problem(s). If not, the lawyer will initiate legal action and have the Trustee explain their actions to the judge. The Trustee can be removed from their post, can be made to pay funds back into the estate, and can be made to have their share reduced, if they are also a beneficiary. Further, if a Trustee has used the funds for their own benefit, they may be criminally liable for theft. The court does not care that the Trustee happens to be the son, because the court will hold the son Trustee to the same standard as a bank Trustee.

8. Real estate problems

   a. Problem properties

Sometimes the land owned by the Trust has problems. It could be a situation where the land is contaminated. In this case, a beneficiary would not want to take title, because their personal name would fall in the chain of title, and they would be personally liable for any contamination problems. The Trustee would be required to either clean the property or sell it with the known defects.

b. Land with title problems or defects

The Trustee is not required to correct any title defects on the property. However, if the Trustee is aware of a title defect, he or she should make it known. If a beneficiary wants the property anyway, the Trustee can grant the property to the beneficiary with the title defects and is not required to cure them. However, most beneficiaries and certainly any new arms-length buyer would not want to take title to property with a known title defect. An example would be where the legal description of the property on a deed is incomplete. Every once in a while, a deed is prepared and the typist mistakenly omits an entire line from the legal description. This means the legal description is defective. Certain times, it may be cured with a scrivener's affidavit saying an error was made. Other times, the title company will want an entire legal proceeding known as a quiet title action done to clear up the title.

c. Uncooperative tenants — the eviction process

The Trustee is occasionally faced with uncooperative tenants occupying property owned by the Trust. This could be a tenant in the property whom mom was trying to evict before her death, or it could be one of the beneficiaries living in one of mom's properties owned by the Trust. This problem happens more often than anyone can imagine. The 45-year old son who has never done anything in his life is living in a house that mom bought. She owns it in the name of the Trust, and it is a Trust asset. He is living there rent free. Mom dies, and now the Trustee must determine what to do. The Trustee has a duty to the other beneficiaries to maximize the value of the asset. A simple solution would obviously be to give the house to that son as part of his share. Unfortunately, in this scenario, the house is worth way more than his share. He does not have any credit, so he cannot receive the house as part of his share and get a mortgage for the balance to pay back to the estate. He does not want to move from the house and in fact he says mom promised him he would get the house, and he would not have to pay money back to the estate. It is the Trustee's duty to hire a lawyer and initiate an eviction proceeding. Since the house is a Trust asset, the

Trustee has a duty to move him out of the house with force, if needed, through the appropriate legal process.

d. Uninsured or underinsured property

An uninsured or underinsured property can become a huge liability for a Trustee. A standard insurance policy on a home will protect against perils, such as fire, theft and some weather damage for the structure(s) and the personal contents. It will also cover medical bills for persons injured on the property and will help protect the Trust against financial loss if it is sued and found legally responsible for a person's injury or property damage.

The Trustee should pay close attention to deductibles, exclusions and limitations of any policy. For example, flood insurance is not part of a standard home insurance contract. It may also be necessary to declare high value items, such as jewelry, if their value exceeds the maximum limit under the standard terms of the policy. If this is not done, you risk being able to claim only a fraction of the value if the item is stolen.

Standard vehicle insurance will protect against accidental damage, fire and theft. It will also provide financial protection against physical damage and/or bodily injury resulting from an accident.

It is the job of the Trustee to determine that all Trust property is properly insured. If it is not and a claim arises, the Trustee may be held personally liable for the damage or a shortfall in coverage resulting from the property being underinsured.

9. Pursuing and defending legal actions — lawsuits

a. Decedent caused an accident and the injured party is now suing.

Dad was driving his car, caused an accident, injured a number of people, and died in the process. The litigation will continue for years and that means the Trust estate will be open for that length of time. Trust estate assets will be subject to liability above and beyond any insurance he had on his motor vehicle, and distributions may be held until litigation is over. A common level of insurance is $100,000 per person and $300,000 per accident. This level of liability insurance is no longer appropriate for most Trust creators. Trust creators should bump up their liability insurance to the next level, which is $300,000 per person and $500,000 per accident. This level of insurance will provide a greater safety net to keep the estate from paying excess jury verdicts. Trust clients are encouraged to consider an umbrella policy which kicks up insurance limits on the home and car to at least $1,000,000 each.

b. The Decedent was killed in an accident and the estate is now suing.

In this scenario, dad was killed in the car accident, and it was someone else's fault. The heirs would have a cause of action to recover for dad's loss of life and other legal remedies. A personal injury lawyer will explain the proper procedure for this type of recovery, which includes opening a probate proceeding. The probate and Trust estates will be open for the entire length of time it takes to settle this personal injury case. It could be between one and three years on average.

c. The Decedent was involved in a lawsuit prior to death.

Occasionally, the decedent will have been involved in some litigation prior to death. It could be a dispute over a fence on the property, a lawsuit involving a broker mishandling the brokerage account, or even a slip and fall at the grocery store. Just because death has occurred, it does not mean the litigation will stop. The personal representative of dad's estate will be substituted as the new party involved in these lawsuits. This substitution should be done within 60 days of death through a document call a suggestion of death. The attorney handling the lawsuit should be informed immediately of dad’s death.

d. Will and Trust contest actions

Will and Trust contest actions are very lengthy and costly. The average Will or Trust contest takes between one and three years and costs between tens of thousands, up to hundreds of thousands of dollars. (See Trust Contest above.)

e. Legal action with beneficiaries regarding the Trust

The beneficiaries are not happy with the way the Trustee has been administering the estate. The Trustee has not been providing appropriate financial information on a timely basis. The Trustee has been spending Trust money for items that are not really beneficial to the Trust or the beneficiaries. The Trustee has been paying for Trustee expenses which the beneficiaries do not believe benefit the Trust in any way. In order to correct these problems, the beneficiaries should first send certified mail to the Trustee identifying these problems. If they are not corrected to the satisfaction of the beneficiaries, they will hire a lawyer and request an accounting be done in front of a judge.

The beneficiaries can question the Trustee on every Trust purchase, sale or expense. The Trustee will have to answer to the court for all of their actions. Any actions deemed by the court to be inappropriate will be set aside. Any expense associated with these transactions could be charged against the Trustee personally, reduce the Trustee's fee, or reduce the Trustee's share of the estate if they are a beneficiary. If the Trustee's actions are highly inappropriate, the court could hold the Trustee personally liable in a criminal manner and have the Trustee charged with theft or impose other criminal sanctions. There are many duties the Trustee must comply with, and they are covered in more detail in a later section titled "Boring but Important Legal Stuff."

10. The Trust appoints one or more other individuals as Co-Trustees

For many situations in life, more is better. However, this does not generally apply to the number of Trustees appointed to administer a Trust. Creators of Trusts request the appointment of successor Co-Trustees for various reasons. Some people request Co-Trustees because they think their children all get along great and should serve together. Others do not want one child to get their feelings hurt or feel left out by not being appointed. Some people believe that having a local Trustee serving with the more business savvy out-of-town Trustee will make the process easier. In the case of blended families and joint planning, one person from each side of the family may be appointed to represent their respective family's interests. Appointing multiple individuals to serve together may very well create larger problems than the ones the Trustor thinks they are solving.

The decision to appoint Co-Trustees should not be based on emotions, age, location or convenience. If everyone gets along, the beneficiaries should have no issue with one being in charge. Sometimes appointing a person so they feel involved, results in a power struggle. The person who has never had a position of authority within the family can decide to take advantage of the situation and try to rule like a tyrant. The local son or daughter may be convenient but may become completely overwhelmed by the responsibility. The one in charge should be the most qualified person who will faithfully administer the Trust, consult with the beneficiaries on major decisions, and act in their best interest. If all of the children are equally capable of serving as Trustee, then name them in age order.

a. How to avoid some Co-Trustee issues

It is often possible for one Co-Trustee to decline to serve and allow the remaining Co-Trustee to solely administer the Trust. If everyone does indeed get along as well as their parents think, there is no reason to complicate the process with more than one Trustee. If two Trustees are deadlocked on an issue, they should first look to the Trust document to see if it provides instruction for dealing with such an issue. If a Trustee has been appointed to serve with one or more Co-Trustees and are unable to resolve an issue, they should seek the advice of a licensed Florida attorney.

b. Co-Trustees agree on all decisions

In the best case scenario, the Co-Trustees get along with each other and are in agreement on all aspects of the administration of the Trust estate. Even in the absence of a disagreement, the process can still take longer in comparison to having a sole successor Trustee. The language in the Trust may allow them to act independently, but that does not mean a bank, broker or title company will not require all Trustees be present to sign the documents. Even with separate signing pages, coordinating with multiple parties and notaries can be time consuming.

c. Co-Trustees disagree but are amicable

Pursuant to Fla. Stat. § 736.0703, Co-Trustees who are unable to reach a unanimous decision may act by majority decision. In situations where there is an odd number of Trustees, this applies and quickly settles most disputes. However, in many situations there are only two Trustees and any disagreement means they are deadlocked. The deadlock can be resolved in a number of manners, depending on the relationship between Trustees. If they have a good working relationship, they may choose to consult the beneficiaries as a tiebreaker, or they can consult their attorney for his or her recommendation. Both of these solutions require the Trustees be willing to accept defeat of their argument.

d. Co-Trustees disagree and are not amicable

Unfortunately, more often than not, neither Trustee is willing to accept defeat. If the Trustees can agree to be bound by the decision of an independent mediator, that person will be presented with both sides of the disagreement, and he or she will issue a ruling. The ruling may be for one side or the other, or somewhere in between. In the worst case scenario, both Trustees hire their own independent lawyers to represent them and advise them of their rights. This may also result in one Co-Trustee petitioning the court to remove the other Co-Trustee. The longer the issue is contested between the Co-Trustees, the more the Trust assets are being depleted by legal fees.

11. Ownership of joint accounts and beneficiary designations

As previously discussed, the Trustee can only control those assets which are titled to the Trust or made payable to the Trust. Under Fla. Stat. § 655.79, accounts that are held jointly with another person are presumed to belong to the surviving joint owner, unless otherwise expressly provided. The presumption created by the statute may be overcome only by proof of fraud, or undue influence, or clear and convincing proof of a contrary intent.

A child is often added to an elderly parent's bank account as a matter of convenience to assist with the paying of bills and other financial transactions. Sometimes, the parent intends for the child to keep the money when they die, and, sometimes, they expect the child to share the funds with the other beneficiaries. In cases where they do not intend for the child to keep the money, more often than not, they do. The longer they have access to the funds, the more they start to think of the money as their own. When they are told by the bank that the account is presumed to belong to them, they claim it as their own. This obviously can cause great angst among the beneficiaries, and, if the Trustee has proof of a contrary intent, he or she must pursue legal action against the joint owner to recover the funds on behalf of the beneficiaries. If the Trustee is unable to legally prove the intent of the Trustor, the child will keep the funds in addition to their share of the Trustor's estate.

One way for a Trustor to avoid this potential problem is to expressly state their intent for all joint accounts to be distributed equally to all beneficiaries at their death, as a bequest in the Trust document. The Trustor should also discuss their intent with the bank to determine the best way to establish the account in the manner they desire. Some institutions offer what is called a convenience account for all deposit accounts, other than a certificate of deposit. The owner establishes it as a single-party account, with one or more individuals designated as agents and the Trust as the beneficiary. The agent has the right to make deposits, withdraw funds, or draw checks on the account, but they have no ownership or beneficiary rights. The Trust gets the account balance at death.

Another potential issue for a Trustee are accounts that are "payable on death" (POD) or "transfer on death" (TOD) to another person. These accounts are not generally considered part of the Trust estate and pass directly to the beneficiary. The beneficiary of a POD or TOD account is also not responsible for contributing to the payment of any debts or taxes owed by the estate. The POD and TOD accounts can result in a disproportionate share of the total estate going to one beneficiary, as well as causing the other beneficiaries' shares to be reduced by debts and taxes.

F. Boring but Important Legal Stuff

A Florida Trustee does not need to be a lawyer or a banker, but the Trustee does need to act with impartiality and a sense of professionalism, since he or she will be held to the same high standard as an institutional bank Trustee. The layman Trustee must comply with required statutory duties. While a Trust is revocable, the duties of the Trustee are owed exclusively to the Trustor. Once the Trust becomes irrevocable, the Trustee has a duty to the qualified beneficiaries. There will most likely be other duties depending on the circumstances of each Trust. The following is not an exhaustive list but encompasses the general duties and statutory provisions that impact most Trust administrations. The Trust document itself should be reviewed for any additional duties required of the Trustee.

If a Trustee has a question, or is unsure of their duties, or a beneficiary complains, the Trustee must seek advice from a licensed Florida attorney.

1. Fiduciary lawyer-client privilege

The fiduciary lawyer-client privilege in Fla. Stat. § 90.5021 applies with respect to the Trustee and any attorney employed by the Trustee. The Trustee wants to make it clear that they, as Trustee, and no one else, are the client of the lawyer hired to assist with the Trust administration and that their communications with the lawyer are privileged and protected from disclosure to the same extent as if the lawyer represented the Trustee personally. Beneficiaries will often mistakenly believe that the lawyer for the Trust represents them and that they have the right to know everything, as well as receive legal advice from the lawyer.

2. Duties to qualified beneficiaries

The Trustee has specific duties to report to the qualified beneficiaries of a Trust. Most administration problems are a direct result of the Trustee failing to properly communicate with the beneficiaries. Providing as much information as possible and keeping the lines of communication open may very well prevent litigation. It is a good idea to send all information to the beneficiaries via a traceable method, so there is a record of when it was mailed and when it was received. Some of the duties owed to qualified beneficiaries are as follows:

a. Within 60 days of an individual accepting to serve as Trustee of a Trust, he or she has a duty to give written notification of the acceptance of the Trust, the full name and address of the Trustee, and the application of the lawyer-client privilege discussed above to the qualified beneficiaries (Fla. Stat. § 736.0813(1)(a)). The beneficiaries have a right to know the person responsible for the management of the Trust and how to contact the Trustee if needed.

b. Within 60 days of the Trustee acquiring knowledge of the creation of an irrevocable Trust or that a formerly revocable Trust has become irrevocable, the Trustee must notify the qualified beneficiaries of the existence of the Trust, the identity of the Trustor, the right to request a copy of the Trust instrument, the right to accountings, and the application of the lawyer-client privilege (Fla. Stat. § 736.0813(1)(b)). In most cases, the revocable Trust becomes irrevocable upon the death of the Trustor.

c. Upon reasonable request, the Trustee shall provide a qualified beneficiary with a complete copy of the Trust instrument (Fla. Stat. § 736.0813(1)(c)).

d. Once the Trust becomes irrevocable, furnish a Trust accounting, as set forth in Fla. Stat. § 736.08135, to the beneficiaries annually as well as on termination of the Trust or on a change of Trustee (Fla. Stat. § 736.0813(1)(d)). The accounting should be prepared in a reasonably understandable report. The accounting must show all cash and property transactions, fees, gains, losses, and receipt and distribution of assets. A qualified beneficiary may waive the Trustee's duty to account to them. If the duty is not waived, the Trustee will want to include limitation language with the accountings.

e. Upon reasonable request, provide qualified beneficiaries with relevant information about the Trust's assets and liabilities, and the particulars of the Trust administration (Fla. Stat. § 736.0813(1)(e)). The more transparent the Trustee makes the process, the better for everyone involved. The Trustee can choose to wait for the information to be requested, or they can provide it on a regular basis.

3. Required actions regarding expenses, claims and assets

a. The Trustee has a duty to pay expenses and obligations to the Trustor's estate, if the Personal Representative makes a written request that such funds are needed (Fla. Stat. § 736.05053).

b. A Florida Trustee has a duty to incur only reasonable expenses, use special skills, and control and protect Trust property. Also, the Trustee must keep accurate records, enforce and defend proper claims, and administer the estate pending the outcome of any Trust contest or other legal proceeding (Fla. Stat. § 736.0805, 736.0806, 736.0809, 736.0810, 736.0811 and 736.08165). The Trustee should carry out the administration of the Trust estate knowing that one day they may have to defend in court every action they have taken in the administration of the estate.

c. A Florida Trustee has a duty not to commingle Trust assets with their own assets (Fla. Stat. § 736.0810(2)). All Trust accounts and assets should always be maintained separately. Even if it would result in a high rate of return for the beneficiaries, there is no instance where the commingling of funds is acceptable.

d. The Trustee must distribute the residuary Trust estate to the proper beneficiaries in a timely manner. Upon termination of the Trust, the Trustee may retain a reasonable reserve for the payment of debts, taxes and expenses (Fla. Stat. § 736.0817). Even at the request of the beneficiaries, the Trustee should not continue to hold assets any longer than absolutely necessary. If the beneficiaries want to continue to hold assets, such as real property, jointly with one another, they need to establish their own entity, such as a limited liability company, for the ongoing management of the assets. The decedent's Trust is not designed for this purpose.

4. Duties governing all actions of the Trustee

a. A Florida Trustee has a mandatory duty to administer the Trust in good faith, in accordance with its terms and purposes, the interests of the beneficiaries, and in accordance with the Florida Trust code (Fla. Stat. § 736.0801).

b. A Florida Trustee has a duty of loyalty and of impartiality. This means the Florida Trustee must administer the Trust solely in the interest of the beneficiaries and administer the Trust impartially, giving due regard to the respective interest of the beneficiaries (Fla. Stat. § 736.0802-3). Generally, this means a Trustee may not participate in any sale or other transaction for his or her own personal account that involves a conflict between his position as Trustee and his fiduciary interest on behalf of the Trust (such as borrowing money from the Trust). All actions by the Trustee must be solely for the benefit of the Trust and not in any way place the Trustee personally in a better position. Any such conflicts of interest between the Trustee and the Trust estate are voidable by the affected beneficiaries. The beneficiaries must assert their right and will be able to set aside any offending transaction.

c. A Florida Trustee has a duty to administer the Trust estate prudently, as a prudent person would, by considering the purposes, terms and distribution requirements, and other circumstances of the Trust, and by exercising his or her reasonable care, skill and caution (Fla. Stat. § 736.0804).

d. The Trustee is personally liable in certain situations if a breach of Trust has occurred. Absent a breach of Trust, a Trustee is not liable to a beneficiary for a loss or depreciation in the value of Trust property or for not having made a profit. (Fla. Stat. § 736.1001-3).

5. Compensation

a. If the terms of a Trust do not specify the Trustee's compensation, a Trustee is entitled to compensation that is reasonable under the circumstances (Fla. Stat. §736.0708).

b. The attorney rendering legal services to the Trustee of a revocable Trust in connection with the initial administration of the Trust, is entitled to reasonable compensation for those legal services. Payment for the services can be made from the assets of the Trust without court order. The attorney's fee for ordinary services may be based on the value of the Trust assets at the time of the Trustor's death and the income earned by the Trust during initial administration. It is presumed to be reasonable at the rate of 75% of the schedule provided for the attorney of a Personal Representative in Fla. Sta. 733.6171. The Trustee and the attorney may also agree to compensation that is determined in another manner or amount.

6. Miscellaneous information

a. The Trustee need not obtain property title insurance until the property is placed up for sale (Fla. Stat. § 736.08105).

b. No bond is required for Trust administration unless the Trust instrument requires it, a beneficiary requests it, or a court determines it is needed to protect the beneficiaries (Fla. Stat. § 736.0702).

c. Any and all Trust disclosure documents, such as a Trust accounting or any other written report of the Trustee, should include limitation language. The limitation notice is a written statement by the Trustee notifying the beneficiary that an action against the Trustee for breach of Trust based on any matter adequately disclosed in a Trust disclosure document may be barred unless the action is commenced within six months after receipt of the Trust disclosure document (Fla. Stat. § 736.1008).

The time limit for a person to bring an action to contest the validity of a Trust that was revocable at the Trustor's death can be reduced to six months if proper notice is given. The Trustee must send the person a copy of the Trust instrument, plus a notice informing them of the Trust's existence, of the Trustee's name and address, and of the time allowed for commencing a proceeding (Fla. Stat. § 736.0604). Six months after receipt of the information, the person is barred from contesting the Trust.

Part Two - Trusts

A. The Living Revocable Trust: Definitions, How They Work, How to Fund Them, and What Happens if they are Not Properly Funded.

1. Definitions

A Living Revocable Trust is a legal document resembling a Will. It contains an individual's instructions for his or her assets in the event of disability and directions for the distribution of assets upon death. After the Trustor creates the Trust, they change the title on their assets from their name individually to their name as Trustee of their Trust. During the Trustor's lifetime, assuming no disability, they control the assets in this Trust. The Trust does not have to file a tax return or pay taxes. The same 1040 tax return they file every year is the same one they use once the Trust has been established. Their social security number is attached to all the assets, and the IRS makes no distinction between them individually and them as Trustee of their Trust for tax purposes. They act as their own Trustee, thus eliminating any professional fees. They can do anything with their assets that they want. **They retain the same control over their assets as they did before the Trust was established**.

An advantage of a Living Revocable Trust is that the assets titled to the Trust do not go through probate upon death. The assets are disposed of more quickly, often at less administrative cost. The successor Trustee is not required to print the public death notice in the newspaper as the Personal Representative may be required to do in probate.

A Living Revocable Trust provides the perfect vehicle for managing the Trustor's assets in the event of their disability. A Will, which functions only in the event of death, carries no such benefit.

REMEMBER: Only those assets titled in the name of the Trust avoid probate. Upon creation of the Trust, the Trustor makes certain the titles to all of the assets are changed to the name of the Trust. If a Trustor neglects to place all their assets in the

Trust, a "Pour-Over Will" will be the controlling legal instrument for any of those assets held outside of the Trust. The Pour-Over Will controls the assets and guides them through probate, so they can be placed directly into the Trust after the probate procedure for those assets has been completed. However, it costs extra money to activate the Pour-Over Will in probate.

2. How a Living Revocable Trust works

When a Living Revocable Trust is created, the legal documents are usually prepared by an attorney. The Trust states the person creating it, the Trustor (also known as the Grantor, Creator or Settlor), and states his or her desire to create a Trust and to also act as the Trustee of the Trust. The Trustor further states that any and all assets that are retitled in the name of the Trust or those which are included in certain scheduled attachments to the Trust become Trust assets. Once the appropriate Trust papers are prepared, the Trustor signs the Trust documents establishing a Living Revocable Trust. After the legal creation of the Trust, the process of funding becomes the next order of business. The funding, described in detail below, is simply the process of retitling the assets from the Trustor's individual name to the Trustor as Trustee of his or her Trust. Once the Trust document has been properly executed and the assets have been retitled and funded into the Trust, those assets in the Trust will avoid probate and guardianship and provide a host of other advantages.

3. Parties to a Living Revocable Trust

One reason why many people are reluctant to create a Living Revocable Trust is because they fear they will lose control of their assets. Nothing could be further from the truth. In certain other Trust arrangements, control of the assets is given up to other people. In many Irrevocable Trusts, for example, a person who creates a Trust simply transfers ownership of their assets to someone else to act as Trustee for the benefit of a third party who has been designated as the beneficiary. In an Irrevocable Trust situation, total control is lost over the asset.

In a Living Revocable Trust document, total control is maintained by the Trustors. If a couple creates the Trust, then they transfer their assets from themselves, individually, to themselves as Trustees. Then, acting as the Trustees, they can manage and control those assets for the benefit of themselves as beneficiaries. In essence, in a Living Revocable Trust document, the persons creating the Trust are the Trustors, the Trustees, and the beneficiaries of the Trust. The same persons control all the assets just as they did prior to the creation of the Trust. And the same applies to single individuals creating their own Trust:

THE TRUSTORS

THE TRUSTEES

THE BENEFICIARIES

There are no restrictions, extra filing fees, tax forms, capital gains taxes, or reappraisal fees.

4. Types of Living Revocable Trusts

The His Trust or Her Trust. The His Trust or Her Trust is a Living Revocable Trust created by one individual. That person is the beneficiary of the Trust during their lifetime. At their death, the successor Trustee distributes the assets of the Trust to the named beneficiaries.

The A/A Trust. The A/A Trust is a joint Living Revocable Trust created by a husband and wife, and they are the beneficiaries during their lives. After the death of the first spouse, the surviving spouse remains the Trustee and sole beneficiary during his or her lifetime. At the death of the surviving spouse, the successor Trustee distributes the assets of the Trust to the named beneficiaries.

The A/B Trust. The A/B Trust is a joint Living Revocable Trust with added tax provisions that provide for the Trust to be divided into two separate Trusts upon the first spouse's death. It is used by a married couple to preserve two unified credit/applicable credit amounts without the need to file a Form 706 tax return. The A Trust can be called the Above Ground Trust for use by the surviving spouse. The B Trust can be referred to as the Below

Ground Trust, indicating the Trust used by the first spouse to die. The surviving spouse has complete access to all funds in the A Trust and limited access to funds in the B Trust. At the death of the surviving spouse, the successor Trustee distributes the assets of the A Trust and the B Trust to the appropriate beneficiaries.

The A/B/C Trust. The A/B/C Trust is like the A/B Trust with added tax provisions that provide for the Trust to be divided into three separate Trusts instead of two. The C Trust is for remaining assets not included in either the A Trust or B Trust so as to allow additional estate tax savings and asset protection. The surviving spouse has complete access to all funds in the A Trust and limited access to funds in the B Trust and C Trust.

The Split Trust. A Split A/B Trust is comprised of two separate Trusts. The wife owns one-half of the estate in her name in her own Trust and the husband owns one-half of the estate in his name in his own Trust. The benefit of this type of Trust is that the accounting is relatively simple. At the death of the Trustor, the Trust becomes irrevocable and may be divided into two separate Trusts depending on the applicable tax exemption and assets held in the Trust at the time of death. The assets should be examined by the successor Trustee to decide which assets should stay in the "Q-Tip" Trust (Trust-A) and which assets should go to the "Credit Shelter" Trust (Trust-B). The “Q-Tip” Trust (Trust-A) is an election made by the successor Trustee to treat the property in this Trust as qualified terminable interest property that qualifies for the marital deduction in the determination of the federal estate tax liability imposed upon the estate. The "Credit Shelter" Trust (Trust-B) is limited to the unified credit equivalent, if no lifetime taxable gifts were made.

5. Advantages of the Living Revocable Trust

a. Avoids probate

The use of this estate planning device helps avoid the cost associated with probate. It also helps to avoid the delay and publicity associated with the probate process. In addition, placing real estate in a Living Revocable Trust also avoids probate in each state where the Trustor owns real property.

b. Avoids guardianship

The Living Revocable Trust prevents guardianship (conservatorship), in the event of physical or mental incapacity. If the Trustor should become incompetent for any reason, the written provisions of the Living Revocable Trust have already provided for appointed backups, so they will not have to go through probate court in order for a guardian to be appointed.

c. Flexible

The Living Revocable Trust is completely flexible. The Trustor can change or cancel it at any time depending on their financial situation or changes in their family relations. One of the most attractive features of a Living Revocable Trust is that it provides the most efficient and effective estate planning process which is not carved in stone. The Trustor can change it as circumstances warrant simply by amending it. They do this by amending the entire Trust document or just one particular section, as needed.

d. Preserves privacy

A Living Revocable Trust preserves privacy. In contrast, the probate process makes all of the decedent's assets, their Will, and all their family matters, financial and personal, open to the public. For $1.00 per page, anyone can obtain a copy of the Will and see whom the decedent has or has not named as the beneficiaries of their estate. By using a Living Revocable Trust, all of the family matters are kept private and confidential.

e. Hard to contest

A Living Revocable Trust is very hard to contest as compared with a Will. In the experience of J. Mark Fisher, P.A., Attorneys at Law, approximately 50% of all contested Wills are done so successfully while very few Living Revocable Trusts have been successfully contested. The difference in contestability arises because a Will is created under testamentary laws, while a Trust is created under the laws of contract. Also, a Will is created at a single moment in time. A Trust, however, is not only created, but it is used on a regular ongoing basis. Courts have ruled that if a decedent used an instrument such as a Trust, then they are presumed to know the contents of it. On the other hand, it is often difficult to prove they knew what was in a Will that they created twenty years ago and have not looked at since the day they signed it.

f. A Living Revocable Trust takes less time

A key problem with probate is the fact it usually takes a long time. With a Living Revocable Trust, disposition can proceed very quickly and efficiently compared with a probate estate. However, certain assets such as real estate may take time to dispose of and therefore lengthen the Living Trust settlement process.

g. Emotional factor

Another negative element of probate arises, because the process is controlled by someone other than the decedent. A judge, an attorney, and the probate court system all become involved. The emotional stress on the family resulting from this process can be devastating. With a Living Revocable Trust, the Trustor is in control of the process. There are certain formalities and requirements that must be met to close or settle a Living Trust estate. However, a family who has set up a Living Revocable Trust is in the driver's seat.

h. Avoids problems of joint ownership

One way to avoid probate is through jointly owning property with someone else. If it is titled properly with joint rights of survivorship, the surviving owner of the property will own the entire parcel without going through the probate process. This method of avoiding probate is potentially hazardous and can leave heirs to face many problems. Owning property through a Living Revocable Trust accomplishes the same thing yet avoids all the problems associated with joint ownership of property.

i. Inexpensive to set up and maintain

A Living Revocable Trust is generally inexpensive to set up and inexpensive to maintain. There are no monthly or yearly fees to pay in order to maintain the Living Revocable Trust. Any changes that are needed can be made through amendments to the Trust. The amendments can be made to one paragraph, one page, or the entire Trust document. Normally, amendments cost approximately $300 depending on the nature of the amendment. Obviously, if a Trustor is amending the entire Trust document, the cost will be greater.

j. Easy disposition of personal tangible property

Most Trust documents provide for the identification of a last separate writing. This last writing enables the creator of the Trust to leave a separate list of personal items to be left to specified beneficiaries. For example, one could leave a list of household items including a crystal vase or baseball card collection and then identify specific people, such as "my daughter, Susie," or "my grandson, Joey," to receive those items. The last dated and signed writing found with the Trust will dispose of all personal property identified in the writing. The Trustor can amend and change this writing every day, if they choose to do so, without having to change the actual wording of the Trust document. Obviously, having a Trust set up in this way provides a tremendous amount of flexibility.

k. Control after death

The use of a Living Revocable Trust allows the Trustor to control their estate after their death. A Will only exists for a specified period of time that ends when all the assets and titles have been transferred. Once the transfers are made, the Will ceases to have any control. Potential problems may occur because the transfers are made to everyone named in the Will, whether they are competent or able to handle the inheritance or not. For example, a Will may say that assets go to son, Tommy. However, Tommy may be two years old at the time of the testator's death. If this occurs, a guardianship estate will be created to manage the funds for Tommy until he reaches the age of 18 years. Upon Tommy's 18th birthday, he will receive all of the money in the account; this may be $10,000 or it may be $10,000,000. Understandably, no one with a sizeable estate would want a large sum of money turned over to a child upon his or her 18th birthday.

One of the goals of a Trust is to provide that minor children do not receive control of their inheritance until they are 25, 30, 35 or whatever age the Trustor selects. This enables the minor child to receive all the necessary financial help from the Trustee. The Trustee can provide for all of the child's needs through college and postgraduate school without leaving the child in complete control of the money when he or she turns 18. Further, if a minor child or other beneficiary were to become incompetent for any reason, the funds could continue to be held in Trust until the incompetent person either becomes competent or passes away. The Trust provides life-long guardianship avoidance for not only the original creators of the Trust but also for all the beneficiaries of the Trust as well.

6. Funding the Living Revocable Trust

Funding the Living Revocable Trust is the critical element when creating a Living Revocable Trust. If the Trust is not properly funded, the Trust will be of little value.

The funding process is not difficult to accomplish or understand. Typically, most people have three "pots" of assets. The first pot holds personal property; this includes tangible items, such as household goods (things in the home), furnishings, jewelry, etc. The second pot contains intangible property, such as stocks, bonds, bank accounts, and things of that nature. The last pot holds the real estate property wherever located.

The process of retitling the assets from the Trustor's individual name to their name as Trustee of the Trust is called "funding." The following are examples of what must be done to transfer particular assets into the Living Revocable Trust, thereby funding the Trust.

a. Bank, savings, and credit union accounts

The mere listing of bank accounts on the transfer of assets schedule attached to the Trust agreement is not sufficient to transfer actual ownership of those accounts. For bank, savings, and credit union accounts to be transferred into the Trust, each institution where such accounts are located must be contacted and arrangements made for the accounts to be re-registered in the Trustee's name. This usually requires the execution of new signature cards by the Trustee. It is important to note the new accounts will continue to use the same Social Security numbers that were on the original accounts. Some banks mistakenly ask the

Trustor to get a separate tax ID number to open this account. If this is done, it is incorrect. The Trustor's Social Security number should be used on all Living Revocable Trust accounts.

Some financial institutions require a copy of the Trust and they may have additional paperwork for the Trustor or their attorney to complete. If the institution says they require closing the existing account and opening a new account to change the title, there are two options: 1) follow that procedure or 2) change the beneficiary on the existing account to the Trust. Remember, the goal is to have all assets owned or payable to the Trust at the Trustor's death to avoid the probate process.

b. Stocks, bonds, and mutual funds

If the Trustor has securities in a brokerage account and those securities are registered in street name (i.e., the broker holds the securities in their account and the client receives a statement), the transfer of those assets is relatively simple. The Trustor instructs the account executive to change the title of the account to the Trustee on behalf of the Trust. An example of the proper manner for taking title to Trust property would be "John Sample and Mary Sample, Trustees of The Sample Living Trust Dated June 19, 2013". The account executive should be given the correct name of the Trustee and told how the account is to be titled. Often, the Trust instrument will specifically state the name of the Trust agreement, in which case that name should be used in identifying the account.

If the Trustor owns securities that are not in a brokerage account, he or she may wish to open a brokerage account and give the securities to the account executive for registration. If for some reason the Trustor does not wish to have a brokerage account, the securities must be sent to the transfer agent of record, along with supporting documentation, such as signed stock powers.

c. Closely-held stock

Stock owned by the Trustor in a closely-held corporation can easily be re-registered to the Trust's name by tendering the stock to the transfer agent along with the necessary stock powers. If this closely held corporation is owned solely by the creator of the Trust, then canceling the original stock certificates and re-issuing them in the name of the Trustee on behalf of the Trust is all that is required to transfer those stock shares into the name of the Trust.

d. Professional service corporations

A professional service corporation is a corporation owned by a professional, such as a certified public account, lawyer, or doctor. A Trustee cannot be the owner of stock in a professional service corporation. Florida Statute 621.09 specifically provides that capital stock in a professional service corporation can be issued only to individuals who are licensed or legally authorized to render professional services. Florida Statute 621.11 further provides that shares in a professional association may be sold or transferred only to another individual who is eligible to become a shareholder of such a corporation.

e. Partnerships

Unless the partnership agreement stipulates otherwise, there is no prohibition against a Trustee also being a partner in a partnership agreement, either limited or general. Moreover, a partner may assign his or her partnership interest and, unless otherwise provided for by another partnership agreement, the assignment does not dissolve the partnership.

f. Life insurance, annuities and qualified plans

The general rule is that a Living Revocable Trust does not become the owner of life insurance, annuities, or qualified plans (401K, IRA, etc.). Normally, these instruments designate beneficiaries upon the Trustor's death. If a husband dies owning life insurance, his wife is generally the beneficiary of the policy. Beneficiaries have also been selected for annuities and qualified plans. Therefore, these assets will always pass outside probate anyway.

One of the few times when life insurance would be retitled in the name of the Trust is when the life insurance policy has a large cash value. Take for example, an estate where the husband and wife are cash poor. The husband, as owner of the life insurance policy, may not die but, rather, becomes incompetent. The wife will have no way of getting to the cash value of the policy to help pay expenses. If that policy is held as an asset of the Trust, then the spouse, as backup Trustee, can step in and use the cash proceeds as needed. In such a case, the Trust will be the first named beneficiary of a life insurance policy. Upon the death of the insured, the proceeds of the life insurance policy will be immediately payable to the Trustee for distribution according to the terms of the Trust. In the case of the married couple, when the husband dies the insurance proceeds will be payable to the wife as the successor Trustee to the Trust. This prevents a situation where the husband and wife both die within a relatively short period of time, and the second-to-die spouse receives the insurance proceeds outside the Trust estate. If this occurs, the insurance proceeds must go through probate before passing to the heirs.

Likewise, tax-deductible annuities and qualified plans normally would not be titled in the name of the Trust. These investments have designated beneficiaries and therefore avoid probate. If these instruments are tax-deferred instruments, the spouse will continue to be listed as the first beneficiary, but the second beneficiary should be changed to the Trustee on behalf of the Trust.

g. Real property

One of the greatest advantages to creating a Living Revocable Trust is the ability to transfer real estate without it going through probate. This specifically includes the transfer of real estate in Florida, as well as every other state where real property is owned by the decedent.

There are many problems associated with the transfer of real estate into a Trust, if it is done by an out-of-state lawyer or by using a "do-it-yourself" form from a generic, "one-size-fits-all" book on Trusts. For instance, in Florida, the home where people live takes on a different legal status than does other real property they own. In Florida, the house is their homestead and they have certain tax advantages and creditor protection rights. If the appropriate language is included, transferring the homestead property into the Living Revocable Trust will not affect their homestead exemption nor will it affect their protection from creditors. Similarly, transferring the property into a Living Revocable Trust will not waive or destroy the $250,000 exemption from capital gains taxes that can be obtained every two years for all homeowners who sell their property. In essence, all the benefits they receive now, by ownership of property, will be maintained even though it is owned by their Living Revocable Trust.

Care should be given to the language of the deed that transfers the property into the Trust, as well as the type of instrument used. Many law firms or out-of-state companies use Quit Claim deeds to transfer real property into the Living Revocable Trust. The problem with using a Quit Claim Deed is that such a deed does not make any warranties of title. This could result in the owner losing any title insurance protection that he previously had. It is preferable to use a Warranty Deed to convey title that normally provides the grantee with prior title warranties.

With only two exceptions, including Alabama, every other state within the United States allows the transfer of property from an individual to an individual's Trust without the payment of documentary transfer stamps. Documentary stamps are the states' tax upon the real estate conveyance. Florida assesses documentary stamps at the rate of $7 per $1,000. That means if the property is worth $1,000, a fee of $7 will be owed in documentary stamps. These stamps are not assessed on property transferred to a Living Revocable Trust. The only fees assessed in Florida are the recording fees and an indexing fee. The recording fees are normally $10 for the first page, $8.50 for additional pages, plus a $.70 minimum in documentary stamps, and a $1 indexing fee for each name on a deed after the first name. If a husband and wife transfer property from themselves, individually, to themselves as Trustees, then the total cost of recording is typically $19.20. In most other states the recording fees vary from $15 to $30 per deed. A few states require small transfer fees that amount to no more than $30 or $40.

Some states, such as Pennsylvania, require the recording of the Trust instrument. The drafting attorney may provide the clients with a summary of the Trust for recording purposes. This allows the Trust to be recorded but keeps the personal information private. There are only a few states that require the recording of the Trust instrument. Most states simply require the recording of the deed and other miscellaneous transfer forms and related documents. Generally, funding a Trust with real estate in the state of Florida takes two to four weeks.

Funding a Trust with real property owned in any other state may take longer depending on that state's requirements and the transfer forms involved. There are forty-nine other states, and each state has numerous counties. (Florida alone has 67 different counties.) These counties operate like little empires, and the recording requirements and necessary forms can vary from county to county within each state. It is best to have either a great deal of patience or to contact a local attorney in the county where the land is located to record the deed to the Trust.

7. What happens if the Trust is not properly funded

    a. Asset invalidly or ineffectively transferred to the Trust

There are a number of ways an asset can be invalidly or ineffectively transferred to a Trust. Some common issues are typographical errors, inadvertent form choices, human error, and ignorance of the law and statutes. While the issue can be easily remedied by the Trustor during their lifetime, the solution is not always easy for the successor Trustee.

Paperwork issues

When funding the Trust, every bank, broker, insurance company and the like have their own forms that must be completed in order to successfully transfer the asset to the Trust or name the Trust as the beneficiary of the asset. A simple typographical error in the name of the Trust or somewhere else on the form can prevent the Trust taking title to the property. The failure of an employee to process the paperwork correctly, or process it at all, may also lead to an ineffective transfer. Depending on the institution and the type of error, there are different solutions.

It may be as easy as showing the Certification of Trust to prove the correct details of the Trust. A Trustee may be able to complete and provide the institution with an affidavit attesting to the correct details and/or the inadvertent error that caused the problem. The worst-case scenario will be that the transfer is set aside and the asset is considered to be held under the previous title. If the asset was in the Trustor's name only with no beneficiary named, the asset will need to be probated as discussed below. If it was jointly owned or payable on death to someone, it will be subject to the laws governing those types of accounts also discussed below.

Homestead property with a surviving spouse or minor children

Article X, Section 4 (c), of the Florida Constitution places restrictions on the devise of Homestead property when it is not owned as tenants by the entireties or as joint tenants with rights of survivorship. The restrictions protect a surviving spouse and/or minor children from losing their homestead property to creditors or other beneficiaries. If a Trustor has minor children, they cannot devise_(direct the disposition of) the homestead property in any manner. If they transfer the homestead property to their Trust and are survived by minor children, the transfer will be deemed invalid and the property will not be a Trust asset.

If the Trustor does not have minor children but is married, they may devise the property to their spouse only. Any document encumbering or transferring the property must be signed by the Trustor and their spouse, regardless of the spouse's ownership interest in the property. A marital contract, such as a prenuptial or postnuptial agreement, can waive the right of the spouse to the homestead property and permit the devise to another person. Absent the appropriate legal waiver of the spouse's rights, the transfer will be deemed invalid and the property will not be a Trust asset. If a Trustee has concerns regarding the validity of a homestead devise, they should contact a licensed Florida attorney.

Real property title or legal description issue

A simple typographical error on a deed is considered harmless but should be corrected. The most common mistakes usually relate to the legal description of the property being transferred. Sometimes numbers are transposed, and other times an entire line of the description may have been skipped. This is what is referred to as a scrivener's error. Once the error is discovered, the person who prepared the document can complete an affidavit. The affidavit will state who they are, what the error was, and the correct legal description.

Other errors are not as easily remedied. If the deed is defective, the decedent did not validly transfer the property to the Trust. The Trustee will need to hire an attorney to open a formal probate proceeding to correct the issue. Only the Personal Representative of the decedent's estate can petition the court to correct the defect. An incomplete Trust name, an insufficient legal description, a lack of an acknowledgement, and the failure of the decedent's spouse to join on the deed transferring their homestead property are a few examples of this type of defect.

b. Asset not transferred to the Trust, not jointly owned, and not payable to a beneficiary

Any asset that is left in the decedent's name only, without a designated beneficiary, will require action by the probate court. Most Trust packages contain what is called a Pour-Over Will. The Pour-Over Will appoints a person to be the Personal Representative of the estate and names the Trust as the sole beneficiary of any probate estate. Once the probate court authorizes distributions to the beneficiary, the assets will be transferred to the Trust and then distributed to the beneficiaries by the Trustee. If a Pour-Over Will is not provided with the Trust, Florida Statute will control the distribution of the asset. Below is a brief description of the three types of court action that may be necessary to retitle the asset.

Disposition of personal property without administration

If the only such asset is exempt personal property (such as household furnishings) or non-exempt personal property that is valued at less than certain funeral and final medical expenses, the court does not require the estate be probated. An informal request can be sent to the court, and, if they are satisfied the asset meets the requirements, they will issue a letter or other writing under the seal of the court, which authorizes the payment, transfer, or disposition of the asset to the appropriate beneficiary.

Summary administration

A summary administration is a shortened probate proceeding that does not require the appointment of a Personal Representative. The petition to begin the administration may be filed by the person appointed as Personal Representative in the Will or any beneficiary. In order to file for summary administration, the decedent must have been dead for more than two years or the value of the probate estate must not exceed $75,000. Assets that are exempt from the claims of creditors, like the homestead property, are not included in the calculation of the value of the probate estate. Once all debts, taxes, and legal fees have been paid, the court will issue an order allowing the assets to be transferred by the Petitioner to the appropriate beneficiary. Typically, the summary administration process is quicker, easier, and less expensive than a formal administration.

Formal administration

A formal administration is the most common type of probate proceeding. A petition to begin the administration is usually filed by the person appointed as Personal Representative in the Will. If that person meets the requirements to serve, the court will accept their petition and issue Letters of Administration that allow the Personal Representative to manage the estate. In the administration process, a decedent's assets are inventoried, and creditors are identified and paid. Once all debts, taxes and legal fees have been paid, the court will authorize the assets to be transferred by the Personal Representative to the appropriate beneficiary. Upon final distribution, the court will issue an order discharging the Personal Representative of his or her duties. The formal administration process is lengthier, closely supervised by the court, more involved, and more expensive than a summary administration.

c. Asset not transferred to the Trust but jointly owned

This type of asset does not require any action by the Trustee and will not be part of the Trust administration. Typically, the surviving joint owner of any financial account need only provide a copy of the decedent's death certificate and proper identification to the institution in order to obtain exclusive ownership of the asset. If the asset is real property owned as joint tenants with rights of survivorship, the recording of the decedent's death certificate and Affidavit of No Florida Estate Tax Due will clear title to the surviving joint owner. If the decedent only added the joint owner to a financial account as a matter of convenience and intended for it to be distributed to all beneficiaries, not just the surviving joint owner, Fla. Stat § 655.79 allows the Trustee to pursue legal action against the joint owner to recover the funds on behalf of the beneficiaries.

d. Asset not transferred to the Trust but payable to a beneficiary

This type of asset also does not require any action by the Trustee and will not be part of the Trust administration. Again, the named beneficiary of any financial account or life insurance policy usually need only provide a copy of the decedent's death certificate and proper identification to the institution in order to obtain exclusive ownership of the asset.

B. Other Types of Trusts

There are numerous types of Trusts in addition to the Living Revocable Trust, described above in Section A. This section provides brief descriptions of many of them.

One major distinction regarding Trusts is whether they are revocable or irrevocable. If one is revocable, that means it is changeable by the maker. If it is irrevocable, the Trust maker cannot change it. In most cases, the Trust maker has passed away and the previously revocable Trust is no longer changeable.

While the maker is living, the maker's Social Security number is the tax identification number for the Trust. Once the maker is gone, then a new identification number is obtained from the IRS. While the maker is living and using their Social Security number, their normal 1040 tax return is used. There is no indication on the tax return a living Trust has been created and no other special forms are needed. Once the Trust maker dies and the new tax identification number is obtained, the Trustee will file any further tax reports using a 1041 tax return.

The majority of Trusts to be administered will be irrevocable Trusts. Even your mother's Living Revocable Trust, once she loses her mental capacity, will be considered an irrevocable Trust. The Florida Statutes impose duties and responsibilities anytime an individual is acting as a Trustee of the Trust, whether it is revocable or irrevocable.

1. The continuing underage child Trust

If a beneficiary of a Trust is under the age of distribution outlined in the Trust agreement, his or her share shall be held and administered as a separate Trust. The document will outline how and when the funds will be distributed to, or on behalf of, the beneficiary. Generally, the Trust will allow funds to be used for the beneficiary's proper care, support, health, maintenance, and education, in their accustomed standard of living. The Trustee is often given the power to pay to or apply for the benefit of such beneficiary, amounts from the principal of the Trust estate up to the whole thereof, as the Trustee may from time to time deem advisable. At such time as the beneficiary attains the age of distribution, the Trustee will distribute to such beneficiary all of the balance of his or her share of the Trust Estate, free of Trust.

2. The continuing Grandchildren's Educational Trust

A set amount or percentage of the Trust estate can be set aside for each of the Trustor's living grandchildren and used for their educational benefit. The Trust will outline any terms the beneficiary must meet in order to receive payments, such as the type of education the funds will be used for or the minimum grade point average the beneficiary must attain. The Trust will also state at what age the remaining principal of the beneficiary's Trust shall be distributed outright to them.

3. The continuing Special Needs Trust

This is a Trust under which the individual is the beneficiary of all or part of the payments from the Trust depending on special needs. The distribution of Trust payments is determined by the Trustee, who uses his or her discretion with regard to the amounts to be distributed to the individual. A properly drafted Special Needs Trust will allow a beneficiary to receive some monetary distributions but not lose Medicaid or SSI benefits.

4. The Qualified Terminable Interest Property Trust (Q-TIP Election)

The Q-TIP Election, commonly known as the Q-TIP Trust, is used primarily for spouses in a second marriage. Its primary purpose is to ensure the new spouse is provided for financially, and the children of the first marriage, if any, inherit the assets from the estate after the death of the new spouse.

5. The Discretionary Trust

A Trust established for an individual and whose distribution is subject to the Trustee's discretion is exempt from garnishment by a creditor. If a Trustee may make discretionary distributions to or for the benefit of the individual, a creditor of the individual, including a beneficiary's child, spouse, or former spouse who has a judgment or court order against the beneficiary for support or maintenance; a judgment creditor who has provided services for the protection of a beneficiary's interest in the Trust; or a claim of this state or the United States to the extent a law of this state or a federal law so provides (Fla. Stat. § 736.0503(2)), may not compel a distribution or attach or otherwise reach the Trust interest (Fla. Stat. § 736.0504).

6. The Spendthrift Provision

A Trust established for an individual which limits that individual's right to the proceeds and provides "spendthrift provisions" is exempt from garnishment by a creditor (Fla. Stat. § 736.0502). These Trusts are not exempt from garnishment actions by a beneficiary's child, spouse, or former spouse who has a judgment or court order against the beneficiary for support or maintenance; a judgment creditor who has provided services for the protection of a beneficiary's interest in the Trust; or a claim of this state or the United States to the extent a law of this state or a federal law so provides (Fla. Stat. § 736.0503(2)). A Discretionary Trust, as outlined above, will shield Trust assets from such creditors.

7. The Irrevocable Life Insurance Trust (ILIT)

The Irrevocable Life Insurance Trust (ILIT) is one of the most powerful tools of an estate planner. The primary asset held by this Irrevocable Trust is life insurance. The Trust is used to remove life insurance death benefits from the insured's gross estate. This allows the full value of the life insurance death benefit to provide liquidity for the payment of estate taxes and administrative expenses.

8. The Personal Residence Income Trust (PRIT)

A Personal Residence Income Trust (PRIT) can be used to remove a large personal asset, namely the home, from the Trustor's taxable estate with only a moderate gift tax cost. This estate planning strategy involves the transfer of personal-use property, the home, to a Trust similar to those described above. The Trustor retains the right to use the asset (analogous to the right to an annual income payment made with a GRAT or GRUT, see below) for a set number of years, after which the asset goes to the persons designated in the Trust agreement (remainder beneficiaries).

9. The Grantor-Retained Annuity Trust (GRAT);

A GRAT is an irrevocable Trust which can be a very effective way to transfer future growth of rapidly appreciating property, at little or no tax cost. The Grantor usually transfers appreciating or income producing property to the Trust and retains the right to receive a fixed annual dollar amount or percentage of the initial assets deposited. The amount will be distributed at least annually from the Trust and provides a steady reliable income stream for the Grantor for a set number of years. Once the Trust is funded with the gift, no additional assets may be transferred to the Trust. When the term of the GRAT ends, the remaining assets are transferred tax-free to the named beneficiaries. If the grantor does not outlive the term of the Trust, all of the property is brought back into the Grantor's estate. In order to be valid, the Trust must comply with the requirements of the Internal Revenue Code. (Caution: A generation-skipping transfer tax is applied on appreciated assets after the annuity expires. As a result, GRATs are not usually used for transfers to grandchildren, only to children.)

10. Grantor-Retained Uni-Trust (GRUT)

A GRUT is an irrevocable Trust, similar to the GRAT discussed above. One difference is that distribution of funds from the GRUT is based on a fixed percentage that is recalculated annually based on the new value of the Trust. Another difference is that the Grantor is allowed to make additional gifts to the Trust after the initial funding.

11. The Grantor Retained Income Trust (GRIT)

A GRIT is an irrevocable Trust that allows the Grantor to receive all of the net income from the Trust assets for a fixed term of years. The net income is distributed to the Grantor annually, or on a more frequent basis, in accordance with the terms of the Trust. At the expiration of the fixed term, the remaining Trust principal is either distributed outright to the beneficiaries or held in Trust for their benefit. If the Grantor survives the term, the principal is excluded from the Grantor's estate for federal estate tax purposes. The primary advantage in establishing a GRIT is that the assets transferred from the Grantor to the GRIT are valued for federal gift tax purposes at a discount. The amount of the discount will depend on the length of the term and the applicable federal rate in effect in the month the GRIT is established.

12. The Qualified Domestic Trust (Q-Dot)

Federal estate tax is imposed on the taxable estate of every citizen of the United States, regardless of where the property is located in the world. The federal estate tax is imposed on the taxable estate of every non-U.S. citizen for property located only in the United States. To prevent a non-citizen spouse from inheriting property from a U.S. citizen and then leaving and removing the property from the United States, the unlimited marital deduction is not available to the non-citizen spouse. Therefore, there will be inheritance taxes due upon the death of the U.S. citizen spouse when a non-citizen spouse is the beneficiary. This special Trust is created to keep the property in the U.S. so it can be taxed. If set up properly, there will be no tax due upon the death of the first spouse. The surviving non-U.S. citizen spouse may use the money as long as it remains in the U.S. and a bank or brokerage firm Trust department is the Trustee.

13. The Rabbi Trust

The Rabbi Trust is an irrevocable Trust that functions as a type of retirement plan or deferred compensation arrangement that offers a limited amount of security to the deferring employee. An employer creates the Trust in order to pay future compensation to employees or independent contractors. The Trust is typically owned by the employer and designed as a Grantor Trust, enabling any Trust income to be taxed to the employer.

14. The Intentionally Defective Grantor Trust (IDGT)

An IDGT is an estate planning tool used to freeze certain assets of an individual for estate tax purposes but not for income tax purposes. The intentionally defective Trust is created as a grantor Trust with an intentional flaw. The flaw guarantees the individual continues to pay income taxes, as income tax laws will not recognize that assets have been transferred away from the individual. The value of the Grantor's estate is reduced by the amount of the asset transferred. The individual will then sell assets to the Trust in exchange for a promissory note of some length, such as 10 or 15 years. The note will pay enough interest to classify the Trust as above market, but the underlying assets are expected to appreciate at a faster rate and not be included in the decedent's estate for estate tax consideration.

15. The Dynasty Trust

The term "Dynasty" Trust is often used to describe a Trust created for the benefit of multiple generations. This Trust is not limited by common law, and in certain states, these Trusts can last forever. Such Trusts are also referred to as "generation-skipping," "mega," or "super" Trusts. The federal transfer tax system is designed to tax property each time it is passed from one generation to the next. To assist in accomplishing this objective, a generation-skipping transfer tax applies an additional penalty tax to the normal gift or estate tax whenever property is transferred to persons two or more generations younger than the transferor, or whenever there are taxable distributions or terminations from the Trust. However, a generation-skipping transfer tax exemption is available, which allows aggregate transfers to be exempt from this tax. This Trust is currently not available in Florida. Florida caps the time limit to 360 years.

16. The Loving Trust

A company that sold Living Revocable Trusts in the 1980s initiated the term "Loving Trust" as a name to be used instead of Living Revocable Trust. The Loving Trust does not, however, differ from a Living Revocable Trust.

17. The Forever Trust

The Forever Trust is similar to a Dynasty Trust, in that the goal is to benefit multiple generations. Many states have what is called the rule against perpetuities, which will dictate the length of time the Trust can continue. The Florida Uniform Statutory Rule Against Perpetuities outlined in Fla. Stat. § 689.225 states that for a nonvested property interest to be valid, the interest must vest or terminate no later than 21 years after the death of an individual then alive, or the interest either vests or terminates within 90 years after its creation. As to any Trust created after December 31, 2000, the

90-year limit has been extended to 360 years. While the Trust in Florida cannot technically continue forever, 360 years is a long time to carry on an estate plan.

18. The Land Trust

The Florida Land Trust is a revocable Trust created by a Grantor for the purpose of buying, holding, financing, and selling Florida real estate or other personal property in a confidential or private manner. The Florida Land Trust Act is outlined in Fla. Stat. § 689.071.

19. The Medicaid Income Qualified Trust (MIQT)

If a person's monthly income exceeds the limit to qualify for Medicaid, an MIQT can be created to retain all excess income in Trust. In order to qualify as an MIQT, the Trust must be irrevocable, declare the State will receive all funds remaining in the Trust at the time of the decedent's death (up to the amount of Medicaid benefits paid on their behalf), consist of their income only, and be signed and dated by the person, their spouse, or a person who has legal authority to act on their behalf or who is acting at their request or the request of their spouse.

20. The Medicaid Asset Protection Trust (MAPT)

The MAPT is an irrevocable Trust created by a Trustor and managed by a Trustee for the Trustor's benefit. The Trustor is entitled to the income; however, they may change the Trustee, they may change the beneficiaries, but they may not access the principal. The transfer of assets to the MAPT are still subject to the Medicaid look-back period of five years. A person's assets, need for assistance, current eligibility status, and many other factors must be considered prior to establishing this type of Trust.

21. The Veterans Asset Protection Trust (VAPT)

The veteran wants to qualify for veteran benefits but is unable to do so because they have assets greater than allowed. In this case, the veteran will transfer their assets to an irrevocable Trust they create. The veteran will have no discretionary rights to take the property back, such as with a Living Revocable Trust. The assets will be irrevocably removed from the veteran's control, but the veteran may have certain rights to income or other limited invasion rights. If set up properly, this particular Trust will allow the veteran to qualify for VA benefits immediately. There is no five-year look back period as with the Medicaid Asset Protection Trust as identified above.

22. Spousal Lifetime Access Trust (SLAT)

The SLAT is an irrevocable Trust created by one spouse for another spouse. It allows the beneficial spouse to receive access to the funds and income, but upon that spouse's death all assets pass directly to the named beneficiaries. This type of Trust is a sophisticated estate tax planning tool used to remove assets from an otherwise taxable estate.

23. The Crummey Trust

A Crummey Trust is an Irrevocable Trust. It allows the Grantor to give assets to the Trust which then owns the assets. Therefore, the assets are no longer included in the Grantor's gross estate. This Trust also holds the assets for the beneficiary until some future date. Normally, the IRS will not allow the Grantor to remove assets from the estate unless the beneficiary has a "present interest" in the property. Holding the property for some future use in the Trust does not satisfy the IRS rules. However, there are exceptions. This type of Trust requires the maker give the beneficiary a window of access to the funds annually deposited to the Trust, such as a 30-day time frame, to take control of those funds. If the beneficiary does not take control of those funds during that 30-day window, the funds continue to be held pursuant to the terms of the Trust. The beneficiary is usually notified of the 30-day window via letter, now commonly called a "Crummey Letter."

24. The Springing Trust

The Springing Trust is used with buy-sell agreements to provide a more equitable distribution between partners. Virtually every buy-sell agreement has a built-in bias in favor of the surviving owner or owners. The use of a Springing Trust provides a technique which can compensate for this built-in bias favoring the surviving owner or owners. It is not necessary to disturb the existing buy-sell agreement, which can be left in place together with current life insurance funding.

25. The 21 Trust

The 21 Trust is used if the Trustor's children are under the age of 21 and they do not want to use the annual gift tax exclusion (or two exclusions, if they and their spouse each give to a child), because a child of tender years may not be able to properly manage the funds. Establishing a 21 Trust allows the Trustor to give the annual gift tax exclusion to a child but retain control of the money until the child reaches the age of 21. If a 21 Trust (originating from IRS code section 2503(C),) is used, than certain criteria must be met before it can qualify for the annual exclusion.

Part Three – Appendix of Example Forms

Figure 1 Trustee Acceptance

Figure 2 IRS-Form SS-4 (Application for Employer Identification Number)

Figure 3 Third Party Authorization

Figure 4 Certification of Trust

Figure 5 Request to Open Safe-Deposit Box

Figure 6 Notice of Trust

Figure 7 Trustee Letter to Beneficiary

Figure 8 Trust Inventory

Figure 9 Affidavit of No Florida Estate Tax Due

Figure 10 Affidavit of Continuous Marriage

Figure 11 IRS Form 56 (Notice Concerning Fiduciary Relationship)

Figure 12 IRS Form 4810 (Request for Prompt Assessment Under Internal Revenue Code Section 6501(d))

Figure 13 IRS Form 5495 (Request for Discharge From Personal Liability Under Internal Revenue Code Section 2204 or 6905)

Figure 14 Trustee's Proposed Plan of Distribution

Figure 15 Partial Receipt and Release and Refunding Agreement

Figure 16 Waiver of Annual/Final Accounting

Figure 17 Trustee's Accounting

Figure 18 No Objection to Annual/Final Accounting

Figure 19 Final Waiver, Receipt, Release and Refunding Agreement

EXAMPLES OF FORMS DISCUSSED IN THE BOOK

The following forms are examples only and should be used solely as a reference. They are not meant to be used in any legal Trust administration. They are not meant to be a substitute or to be used in place of a Trust attorney's assistance. The case law, statutes and county administration rules may add additional forms not covered in this book or may have changed the nature of the forms outlined in this book. The forms have been completed for fictitious clients John and Mary Sample. The Trustee is referred to as Daughter Sample.

Figure 1 Trustee Acceptance

THE SAMPLE LIVING TRUST DATED FEBRUARY 1, 1999

ACCEPTANCE OF DAUGHTER SAMPLE AS SUCCESSOR TRUSTEE

WHEREAS, **JOHN SAMPLE and MARY SAMPLE**, as Trustors, entered into **THE SAMPLE LIVING TRUST DATED FEBRUARY 1, 1999**, designating themselves as Trustees; and

WHEREAS, **JOHN SAMPLE** died on June 1, 2007; and

WHEREAS, **MARY SAMPLE** died on January 12, 2017; and

WHEREAS, under Article VII of the Agreement, **DAUGHTER SAMPLE** is nominated to serve as the Successor Trustee.

NOW THEREFORE, **DAUGHTER SAMPLE** hereby accepts the appointment to serve as sole Successor Trustee of **THE SAMPLE LIVING TRUST DATED FEBRUARY 1, 1999**.

EXECUTED this January 31, 2017.

____
DAUGHTER SAMPLE
123 Government Street
Pensacola, FL 32502

STATE OF FLORIDA
COUNTY OF OKALOOSA

The foregoing instrument was acknowledged before me on January 31, 2017, by **DAUGHTER SAMPLE**, who is personally known to me or who has produced ________________________ as identification and who did not take an oath.

____
Notary Public

Seal and Commission
Expiration Stamp:

States the person appointed has accepted to serve as Trustee

Figure 2 IRS-Form SS-4 (Application for Employer Identification Number)

Form **SS-4** (Rev. January 2010) Department of the Treasury Internal Revenue Service

Application for Employer Identification Number

(For use by employers, corporations, partnerships, trusts, estates, churches, government agencies, Indian tribal entities, certain individuals, and others.)

▶ See separate instructions for each line. ▶ Keep a copy for your records.

OMB No. 1545-0003

EIN

Type or print clearly.

1 Legal name of entity (or individual) for whom the EIN is being requested

2 Trade name of business (if different from name on line 1)

3 Executor, administrator, trustee, "care of" name

4a Mailing address (room, apt., suite no. and street, or P.O. box)

5a Street address (if different) (Do not enter a P.O. box.)

4b City, state, and ZIP code (if foreign, see instructions)

5b City, state, and ZIP code (if foreign, see instructions)

6 County and state where principal business is located

7a Name of responsible party

7b SSN, ITIN, or EIN

8a Is this application for a limited liability company (LLC) (or a foreign equivalent)? . . . . ☐ Yes ☐ No

8b If 8a is "Yes," enter the number of LLC members . . . . ▶

8c If 8a is "Yes," was the LLC organized in the United States? . . . . ☐ Yes ☐ No

9a **Type of entity** (check only one box). **Caution.** If 8a is "Yes," see the instructions for the correct box to check.

☐ Sole proprietor (SSN) ______
☐ Partnership
☐ Corporation (enter form number to be filed) ▶ ______
☐ Personal service corporation
☐ Church or church-controlled organization
☐ Other nonprofit organization (specify) ▶ ______
☐ Other (specify) ▶
☐ Estate (SSN of decedent) ______
☐ Plan administrator (TIN) ______
☐ Trust (TIN of grantor) ______
☐ National Guard ☐ State/local government
☐ Farmers' cooperative ☐ Federal government/military
☐ REMIC ☐ Indian tribal governments/enterprises
Group Exemption Number (GEN) if any ▶

9b If a corporation, name the state or foreign country (if applicable) where incorporated | State | Foreign country

10 **Reason for applying** (check only one box)

☐ Started new business (specify type) ▶ ______
☐ Hired employees (Check the box and see line 13.)
☐ Compliance with IRS withholding regulations
☐ Other (specify) ▶
☐ Banking purpose (specify purpose) ▶ ______
☐ Changed type of organization (specify new type) ▶ ______
☐ Purchased going business
☐ Created a trust (specify type) ▶ ______
☐ Created a pension plan (specify type) ▶ ______

11 Date business started or acquired (month, day, year). See instructions.

12 Closing month of accounting year

13 Highest number of employees expected in the next 12 months (enter -0- if none). If no employees expected, skip line 14.

Agricultural	Household	Other

14 If you expect your employment tax liability to be $1,000 or less in a full calendar year **and** want to file Form 944 annually instead of Forms 941 quarterly, check here. (Your employment tax liability generally will be $1,000 or less if you expect to pay $4,000 or less in total wages.) If you do not check this box, you must file Form 941 for every quarter. ☐

15 First date wages or annuities were paid (month, day, year). **Note.** If applicant is a withholding agent, enter date income will first be paid to nonresident alien (month, day, year) . . . . ▶

16 Check **one** box that best describes the principal activity of your business. ☐ Health care & social assistance ☐ Wholesale-agent/broker
☐ Construction ☐ Rental & leasing ☐ Transportation & warehousing ☐ Accommodation & food service ☐ Wholesale-other ☐ Retail
☐ Real estate ☐ Manufacturing ☐ Finance & insurance ☐ Other (specify)

17 Indicate principal line of merchandise sold, specific construction work done, products produced, or services provided.

18 Has the applicant entity shown on line 1 ever applied for and received an EIN? ☐ Yes ☐ No
If "Yes," write previous EIN here ▶

Third Party Designee

Complete this section **only** if you want to authorize the named individual to receive the entity's EIN and answer questions about the completion of this form.

Designee's name — Designee's telephone number (include area code) ( )

Address and ZIP code — Designee's fax number (include area code) ( )

Under penalties of perjury, I declare that I have examined this application, and to the best of my knowledge and belief, it is true, correct, and complete.

Name and title (type or print clearly) ▶ — Applicant's telephone number (include area code) ( )

Applicant's fax number (include area code) ( )

Signature ▶ Date ▶

For Privacy Act and Paperwork Reduction Act Notice, see separate instructions. Cat. No. 16055N Form **SS-4** (Rev. 1-2010)

Allows the Trustee to apply for an EIN to replace the deceased Trustor's social security number

Figure 3 Third Party Authorization

ONLINE EMPLOYER IDENTIFICATION NUMBER APPLICATION

THIRD PARTY DESIGNEE AUTHORIZATION

AUTHORIZATION BY SUCCESSOR TRUSTEE
AND/OR PERSONAL REPRESENTATIVE

THE UNDERSIGNED, **DAUGHTER SAMPLE**, does hereby understand and authorize **ATTORNEY** to apply for and receive an Employer Identification Number on my behalf for **THE SAMPLE LIVING TRUST DATED FEBRUARY 1, 1999**.

EXECUTED this January 31, 2017.

____
DAUGHTER SAMPLE

Allows a third party to apply for the EIN online on behalf of the Trustee

Figure 4 Certification of Trust

CERTIFICATION OF TRUST

Trustors: **JOHN SAMPLE and MARY SAMPLE**
Name of Trust: **THE SAMPLE LIVING TRUST**
Date of Trust: **FEBRUARY 1, 1999**
Date of First Amendment: **DECEMBER 3, 2008**
Current Trustee: **DAUGHTER SAMPLE**
Address of Current Trustee: **123 Government Street, Pensacola, FL 32502**
Successor Trustee: **SON SAMPLE**
Trust Tax Identification Number: **00-00000000**

The undersigned **DAUGHTER SAMPLE** does hereby confirm the existence of the within-described Trust and certify, under penalty of perjury, the following pursuant to Florida Statute 736.1017:

1. The undersigned is the sole currently serving Trustee. The signature of the above named Trustee is required for any action taken on behalf of the Trust.

2. The Trust is in full force and effect and has not been revoked, terminated, or otherwise amended in any manner which would cause the representation in this Certification of Trust to be incorrect.

3. The Trust is irrevocable.

4. The above-designated Trustee is fully empowered to act for said Trust and is properly exercising the Trustee's authority under this Trust. No other Trustee or other individual or entity is required to execute any document for the Trust.

5. The proper manner for taking title to Trust property is: **DAUGHTER SAMPLE, TRUSTEE OF THE SAMPLE LIVING TRUST DATED FEBRUARY 1, 1999.**

6. To the undersigned's knowledge, there are no claims, challenges of any kind, or causes of action alleged, which contest or question the validity of the Trust or the Trustee's authority to act for the Trust.

7. The Trustee is authorized by the Trust Agreement to contract for the purchase of, option, purchase, sell, convey, borrow, pledge, mortgage, lease, operate, control, transfer title to, and divide Trust property, both real and personal property, both tangible and intangible including but not limited to securities, real property and accounts of all kinds. This authority specifically extends to checking accounts, savings accounts, money market, certificates of deposit, deeds, mortgages, certifications, affidavits, closing statements and all other related closing documents and such instruments as may be necessary to carry out the purposes and intents of this Trust.

8. Attached to the Certification of Trust is a copy of the death certificates of **JOHN SAMPLE and MARY SAMPLE.**

IN WITNESS WHEREOF: the undersigned, being the Trustee, does hereby execute this Certification of Trust this January 31, 2017.

Witnesses: Trustee:

__________________________ __________________________

Witness **DAUGHTER SAMPLE**

____

Witness

STATE OF FLORIDA
COUNTY OF OKALOOSA

The foregoing instrument was acknowledged before me on January 31, 2017, by **DAUGHTER SAMPLE**, who is personally known to me or who has produced ______________________ as identification and who did not take an oath.

____

Notary Public

A short form that can be furnished by the Trustee to a third party. The form must contain specific details of the Trust but need not include the distribution.

Figure 5 Request to Open Safe-Deposit Box

____

____

____

____

Re: Request to Open Safe-Deposit Box and Examine Contents Pursuant to Fla. Stat. §655.935 Search Procedure on Death of Lessee

Gentlemen/Ladies:

MARY SAMPLE, was the lessee of safe-deposit box #1450, leased by ABC Bank as lessor. **MARY SAMPLE** died on January 12, 2017, as proven by the attached death certificate. No court order has been issued to open and examine the contents of box #1450. I am the spouse/parent/adult descendant/Personal Representative and hereby request to open and examine the contents of the safe-deposit box leased or co-leased by **MARY SAMPLE**, or any document(s) delivered by **MARY SAMPLE** for safekeeping.

I understand an officer of your institution shall remove and deliver only the following documents:

1. Any writing purporting to be a Will of the decedent, to the court having probate jurisdiction in the county in which the financial institution is located.
2. Any writing purporting to be a deed to a burial plot or to give burial instructions, to the person making the request for a search.
3. Any document purporting to be an insurance policy on the life of the decedent, to the beneficiary named therein.

I further understand you shall make a complete copy of any document removed and delivered and place that copy, together with a memorandum of delivery, in the safe deposit box leased by the decedent.

Sincerely,

DAUGHTER SAMPLE

Allows the authorized person to view and remove certain documents

Figure 6 Notice of Trust

IN THE CIRCUIT COURT FOR OKALOOSA COUNTY, FLORIDA

IN RE:	ESTATE OF MARY SAMPLE #222-22-2222	PROBATE DIVISION File Number ____________

Deceased.

Division ____________

NOTICE OF TRUST

MARY SAMPLE, a resident of Okaloosa County, Florida, who died on January 12, 2017, was the Trustor of a Trust entitled: **THE SAMPLE LIVING TRUST DATED FEBRUARY 1, 1999**, which is a Trust described in Section 733.707(3) of the Florida Statutes, and is liable for the expenses of the administration of the decedent's estate and enforceable claims of the decedent's creditors to the extent the decedent's estate is insufficient to pay them, as provided in section 733.607(2) of the Florida Statutes.

The name and address of the Trustee is set forth below.

The clerk shall file and index this Notice of Trust in the same manner as a caveat, unless there exists a probate proceeding for the Trustor's estate in which case this Notice of Trust must be filed in the probate proceeding and the clerk shall send a copy to the Personal Representative.

EXECUTED this January 31, 2017.

____

DAUGHTER SAMPLE, Trustee
123 Government Street
Pensacola, FL 32502
334-804-5252

Copy mailed to attorney for the Personal Representative on
____________, 20__.
CLERK OF THE CIRCUIT COURT

By:
Mail to:

Must be filed with the County to identify the deceased Trustor and the Successor Trustee

Figure 7 Trustee Letter to Beneficiary

____

Sent via certified mail, return receipt requested, via article no. _______________

Son Sample
555 Sample Street
Destin, FL 32548

RE: THE SAMPLE LIVING TRUST DATED FEBRUARY 1, 1999

Dear Son Sample:

This letter is to notify you of the death of Mary Sample on January 12, 2017. Mary Sample was the Trustor of The Sample Living Trust Dated February 1, 1999. You are a qualified beneficiary of this Trust and in accordance with Florida Statute 736.0813 and 736.0604(2), I am informing you of the following:

1. I, Daughter Sample, have formally agreed to serve as the Successor Trustee of The Sample Living Trust Dated February 1, 1999. Enclosed is a copy of the acceptance, which identifies my mailing address as 123 Government Street, Pensacola, FL 32502.
2. The acting Trustee shall provide a Trust accounting, as set forth in Florida Statute 736.08135, annually and on termination of the Trust or on change of the Trustee.
3. Upon reasonable request, the acting Trustee shall provide relevant information about the assets and liabilities of the Trust and the particulars relating to administration.
4. A copy of the Trust instrument, a notice of the Trust's existence and the Trustees' names and addresses are enclosed.
5. An action to contest the validity of the Trust is limited to six (6) months from the date this notice was sent.
6. The fiduciary lawyer-client privilege in Florida Statute 90.5021 applies with respect to the Trustee and any attorney employed by the Trustee.

Under the terms of the Trust, the Trust became irrevocable upon the death of Mary Sample. It is the Successor Trustee's job to promptly distribute Trust assets to the beneficiaries in accordance with the terms of the Trust. The assets cannot be distributed until all debts (including taxes) have been paid. You will be contacted as soon as all debts have been satisfied and distributions can be made.

You have the right to waive the Trustee's duty to provide an annual accounting to you. If you would like to exercise this right, please sign the enclosed waivers in the presence of a notary public, and mail back to me at the address cited above.

If you have any questions regarding the administration of the Trust, please feel free to contact me.

Sincerely,

Daughter Sample

Daughter Sample

Enc: Acceptance, Notice of Trust, copy of the Trust and Waivers of Annual and Final Accounting
cc: File, Trustee

Satisfies the Trustee's duty to inform the beneficiaries of certain statutory requirements

Figure 8 Trust Inventory

THE SAMPLE LIVING TRUST DATED FEBRUARY 1, 1999 INVENTORY OF TRUST ASSETS			
Asset Description (car, boat, bank accounts, brokerage accounts, IRA's, annuities, property, etc.)	**Asset Location** (Name of Bank or Financial Institution where asset is held or physical location)	**How is asset titled?** Provide proof by attaching statement or copy of deed as of date of death	**Copy of document attached** (car title, bank statement, etc.) ✓

A list of all assets and liabilities that can be given to the beneficiaries

Figure 9 Affidavit of No Florida Estate Tax Due

FLORIDA
Department of Revenue

Affidavit of No Florida Estate Tax Due

DR-312
R. 08/13
TC
Rule 12C-3.008
Florida Administrative Code
Effective 01/14

(This space available for case style of estate probate proceeding)

(For official use only)

State of ____________________ County of ____________________

I, the undersigned, ______________________________ (print name of personal representative), do hereby state:

1. I am the personal representative as defined in section 198.01 or section 731.201, Florida Statutes, as the case may be, of the estate of ______________________________ (print name of decedent).
2. The decedent referenced above died on ____/____/____ (date of death), and was domiciled (as defined in s. 198.015, F.S.) at the time of death in the state of ____________________.

   On date of death, the decedent was (check one): ☐ a U.S. citizen ☐ **not** a U.S. citizen
3. A federal estate tax return (federal Form 706 or 706-NA) is not required to be filed for the estate.
4. The estate does not owe Florida estate tax pursuant to Chapter 198, F.S.
5. I acknowledge personal liability for distribution in whole or in part of any of the estate by having obtained release of such property from the lien of the Florida estate tax.

Under penalties of perjury, I declare that I have read this Affidavit and the facts stated in it are true. This declaration is based on all information of which the personal representative has any knowledge [ss. 92.525(1)(b); 213.37; 837.06, F.S.].

Executed this ______ day of ____________, 20______ Signature ____________________

Print name ____________________ Telephone number ____________________

Mailing address ____________________ City/State/ZIP ____________________

State of ____________________ County of ____________________

Sworn to (or affirmed) and subscribed before me by ______________________________

On this__________ day of ____________, 20__________

Signature of Notary ____________________

(Check one)

☐ Personally known

☐ Or produced identification

Type of identification produced ____________________

____
Print, type, or stamp name of Notary Public

File this form with the appropriate clerk of the court. Do not mail to the Florida Department of Revenue.

Recorded in each county where property is owned to show there is no tax liability which could result in a lien on the property

Figure 10 Affidavit of Continuous Marriage

STATE OF FLORIDA
COUNTY OF OKALOOSA

AFFIDAVIT OF CONTINUOUS MARRIAGE

Before me, the undersigned authority, personally appeared **DAUGHTER SAMPLE**, the undersigned party who has executed this Affidavit, who made the following statements:

1. **Purpose of Affidavit.** I am making this Affidavit based upon my personal knowledge for the purpose of establishing the facts set forth below.

2. **Continuous Marriage. MARY SAMPLE**, was married to **JOHN SAMPLE** on May 1, 1945, and was continuously married during the time of conveyance of the land described in the Deed recorded in Official Records Book 0000, Page 0000, of the public records of Okaloosa County and they did remain married to the other at all times thereafter until the death of **MARY SAMPLE** at Okaloosa County on January 12, 2017. The subject property is more particularly described as:

Parcel #: 123-45-678-91011

3. **Attachment**. Attached to the Affidavit is a copy of the death certificate of **MARY SAMPLE.**

____
DAUGHTER SAMPLE, Trustee
123 Government Street
Pensacola, FL 32502
334-804-5252

STATE OF FLORIDA
COUNTY OF OKALOOSA

The foregoing instrument was sworn to and subscribed before me this January 31, 2017, by **DAUGHTER SAMPLE,** who is personally known to me and who did take an oath.

____
Notary Public

Notary Seal and commission
expiration stamp:

Clears the title of real property to the surviving spouse

Figure 11 IRS Form 56 (Notice Concerning Fiduciary Relationship)

Form **56**
(Rev. December 2015)
Department of the Treasury
Internal Revenue Service

Notice Concerning Fiduciary Relationship

► Information about Form 56 and its separate instructions is at *www.irs.gov/form56*.
(Internal Revenue Code sections 6036 and 6903)

OMB No. 1545-0013

Part I Identification

Name of person for whom you are acting (as shown on the tax return)	Identifying number	**Decedent's social security no.**

Address of person for whom you are acting (number, street, and room or suite no.)

City or town, state, and ZIP code (If a foreign address, see instructions.)

Fiduciary's name

Address of fiduciary (number, street, and room or suite no.)

City or town, state, and ZIP code	Telephone number (optional) ( )

Section A. Authority

1 Authority for fiduciary relationship. Check applicable box:
- a ☐ Court appointment of testate estate (valid will exists)
- b ☐ Court appointment of intestate estate (no valid will exists)
- c ☐ Court appointment as guardian or conservator
- d ☐ Valid trust instrument and amendments
- e ☐ Bankruptcy or assignment for the benefit or creditors
- f ☐ Other. Describe ► ______

2a If box 1a or 1b is checked, enter the date of death ► ______
b If box 1c—1f is checked, enter the date of appointment, taking office, or assignment or transfer of assets ► ______

Section B. Nature of Liability and Tax Notices

3 Type of taxes (check all that apply): ☐ Income ☐ Gift ☐ Estate ☐ Generation-skipping transfer ☐ Employment ☐ Excise ☐ Other (describe) ► ______

4 Federal tax form number (check all that apply): **a**☐ 706 series **b**☐ 709 **c**☐ 940 **d**☐ 941, 943, 944 **e**☐ 1040, 1040-A, or 1040-EZ **f** ☐ 1041 **g**☐ 1120 **h**☐ Other (list) ► ______

5 If your authority as a fiduciary does not cover all years or tax periods, check here . . . . ► ☐
and list the specific years or periods ► ______

6 If the fiduciary has a CAF number and wants a copy of notices and correspondence **(see the instructions)** check this box . ► ☐
and enter the year(s) or period(s) for the corresponding line 4 item checked. If more than one form entered on line 4h, enter the form number.

Complete only if the line 6 box is checked.

If this item is checked:	Enter year(s) or period(s)	If this item is checked:	Enter year(s) or period(s)
4a		4b	
4c		4d	
4e		4f	
4g		4h:	
4h:		4h:	

For Paperwork Reduction Act and Privacy Act Notice, see separate instructions. Cat. No. 16375I Form **56** (Rev. 12-2015)

Form 56 (Rev. 12-2015) Page **2**

Part II **Revocation or Termination of Notice**

Section A—Total Revocation or Termination

7 Check this box if you are revoking or terminating all prior notices concerning fiduciary relationships on file with the Internal Revenue Service for the same tax matters and years or periods covered by this notice concerning fiduciary relationship ▶ ☐

Reason for termination of fiduciary relationship. Check applicable box:

a ☐ Court order revoking fiduciary authority

b ☐ Certificate of dissolution or termination of a business entity

c ☐ Other. Describe ▶

Section B—Partial Revocation

8a Check this box if you are revoking earlier notices concerning fiduciary relationships on file with the Internal Revenue Service for the same tax matters and years or periods covered by this notice concerning fiduciary relationship . . . . ▶ ☐

b Specify to whom granted, date, and address, including ZIP code.

▶

Section C—Substitute Fiduciary

9 Check this box if a new fiduciary or fiduciaries have been or will be substituted for the revoking or terminating fiduciary and specify the name(s) and address(es), including ZIP code(s), of the new fiduciary(ies) . . . . ▶ ☐

▶

Part III **Court and Administrative Proceedings**

Name of court (if other than a court proceeding, identify the type of proceeding and name of agency)		Date proceeding initiated	
Address of court		Docket number of proceeding	
City or town, state, and ZIP code	Date	Time ☐ a.m. ☐ p.m.	Place of other proceedings

Part IV **Signature**

Please Sign Here

I certify that I have the authority to execute this notice concerning fiduciary relationship on behalf of the taxpayer.

▶ Fiduciary's signature | Title, if applicable | Date

Form **56** (Rev. 12-2015)

Informs the IRS the Successor Trustee is the contact person for the Trust and informs the IRS when the Successor Trustee is no longer the contact person for the Trust

Figure 12 IRS Form 4810 (Request for Prompt Assessment Under Internal Revenue Code Section 6501(d))

Form **4810** (Rev. February 2009) Department of the Treasury Internal Revenue Service

Request for Prompt Assessment Under Internal Revenue Code Section 6501(d)

► **See instructions on back.**

OMB No. 1545-0430

For IRS Use Only

Requester's name

Title

Kind of tax

☐ Income
☐ Gift
☐ Employment
☐ Excise

Number, street, and room or suite no. (If a P.O. box, see instructions.)

City, town, or post office, state, and ZIP code

Daytime phone number

Tax Returns for Which Prompt Assessment of Any Additional Tax is Requested

Form Number	Tax Period Ended	SSN/EIN on Return	Name and Address Shown on Return	Service Center Where Filed	Date Filed

If applicable, provide the name of decedent's spouse (surviving or deceased)

Spouse's social security number

If corporate income tax returns are included, check the applicable box below:

☐ Dissolution has been completed.
☐ Dissolution has begun and will be completed either before or after the 18-month period of limitation.
☐ Dissolution has not begun but will begin before the 18-month period of limitation expires and will be completed either before or after that period expires.

Attached are copies of:

☐ The returns listed above.
☐ Letters of administration or letters testamentary.
☐ Other (describe):

I request a prompt assessment of any additional tax for the kind of tax and periods shown above, as provided by Internal Revenue Code section 6501(d).

Sign Here

Under penalties of perjury, I declare that I have examined this request, including accompanying schedules and statements, and to the best of my knowledge and belief, it is true, correct, and complete.

☐ **I certify that I have never been assessed any penalties for civil fraud for any federal or state tax matter nor have I been charged with, indicted for, or convicted of fraud. If you cannot certify this statement, attach a detailed statement explaining the circumstances under which you were assessed a penalty, charged with, indicted for, or convicted of fraud.**

▶ Signature of requester | Date | ▶ Identifying number

For Privacy Act and Paperwork Reduction Act Notice, see back of form. Cat. No. 42022S Form **4810** (Rev. 2-2009)

Requests the IRS review the estate for tax liabilities

Figure 13 IRS Form 5495 (Request for Discharge From Personal Liability Under Internal Revenue Code Section 2204 or 6905)

Form **5495**
(Rev. December 2008)
Department of the Treasury
Internal Revenue Service

Request for Discharge From Personal Liability Under Internal Revenue Code Section 2204 or 6905

▶ See instructions on back.

OMB No. 1545-0432

For IRS Use Only

Decedent's name | Date of death | **Social security number**

Requester's name

Title

Number, street, and room or suite no. (If a P.O. box, see instructions.)

City, town, or post office, state, and ZIP code

Kind of Tax
☐ Income
☐ Gift
☐ Estate

Daytime phone number

Tax Returns for Which Discharge From Personal Liability is Requested

Form Number	Tax Period Ended	SSN/EIN on Return	Name and Address Shown on Return	Service Center Where Filed	Date Filed

If applicable, provide the name of the decedent's spouse (surviving or deceased) | **Spouse's social security number**

I have attached the items checked to help expedite action on my request.

☐ Copies of returns listed above.
☐ Copies of letters of administration or letters testamentary.
☐ Other (describe):

I request a discharge from personal liability for any deficiency for the kind of tax and periods shown above, as provided by section 2204 or 6905 of the Internal Revenue Code.

Sign Here

Under penalties of perjury, I declare that I have examined this request, including accompanying schedules and statements, and to the best of my knowledge and belief, it is true, correct, and complete.

☐ **I certify that I have never been assessed any penalties for civil fraud for any federal or state tax matter nor have I been charged with, indicted for, or convicted of fraud. If you cannot certify this statement, attach a detailed statement explaining the circumstances under which you were assessed a penalty, charged with, indicted for, or convicted of fraud.**

▶ Signature of requester | Date | ▶ Identifying number

For Privacy Act and Paperwork Reduction Act Notice, see back of form. Cat. No. 42571S Form **5495** (Rev. 12-2008)

Requests the IRS release the Trustee from liability related to the estate

Figure 14 Trustee's Proposed Plan of Distribution

THE SAMPLE LIVING TRUST DATED FEBRUARY 1, 1999

PROPOSED PLAN OF DISTRIBUTION

Account balance as of December 31, 2017 (actual balance may be slightly different at the time of distribution)		$319,200.00
Less Anticipated Final Expenses:		
Accounting and tax fees:		($10,000.00)
Attorney fees:		($1,200.00)
Administration fees:		($31,920.00)
Approximate balance to be distributed:		**$276,080.00**
SON SAMPLE	50%	$138,040.00
DAUGHTER SAMPLE	50%	$138,040.00

The anticipated accounting fees ($10,000) held for taxes for 2017 shall be held until those taxes have been filed, no later than April 2018. Any funds remaining after taxes and expenses shall be distributed equally, among the beneficiaries.

Trustee: Date:

DAUGHTER SAMPLE

Pursuant to Florida Statute 736.1008, an action for breach of trust based on matters disclosed in a trust accounting or other written report of the trustee may be subject to a 6-month statute of limitations from the receipt of the trust accounting or other written report. If you have questions, please consult your attorney.

Informs the beneficiaries how the Trustee intends to distribute the estate

Figure 15 Partial Receipt and Release and Refunding Agreement

PARTIAL DISTRIBUTION
RECEIPT AND RELEASE AND REFUNDING AGREEMENT

IN RE: **THE SAMPLE LIVING TRUST DATED FEBRUARY 1, 1999**

The undersigned, **SON SAMPLE**, does hereby:

1. Acknowledge that **DAUGHTER SAMPLE**, Trustee of the above referenced Trust, has delivered the following property to the undersigned, **SON SAMPLE**, beneficiary of **THE SAMPLE LIVING TRUST DATED FEBRUARY 1, 1999**:

    - **$10,000 (TEN THOUSAND DOLLARS)**

2. Acknowledge the above-described property as partial distribution from the Trust.

3. Release discharge, and agree to hold harmless **DAUGHTER SAMPLE**, from any further accountability and liability in connection with said property.

4. Agree, in consideration of the delivery of said property, that if any claims, and fiduciaries' compensation become properly payable by the Trustee out of the said property, the undersigned will, immediately upon demand, pay over the amount thereof to the Trustee or retransfer and redeliver to the Trustee for sale and liquidation such part of the said property as the Trustee shall demand.

This the ______________ day of ________________, 20____.

____
SON SAMPLE, Beneficiary

Signed by a beneficiary to acknowledge they have received a portion of their share from the Trustee

Figure 16 Waiver of Annual/Final Accounting

WAIVER OF ANNUAL/FINAL ACCOUNTING

Pursuant to Florida Statute 736.0813(2), I, **SON SAMPLE**, as a qualified beneficiary of **THE SAMPLE LIVING TRUST DATED FEBRUARY 1, 1999**, hereby waive the Trustee's duty to provide me with future annual accountings/a final accounting as set forth under Florida Statute 736.0813(1)(d).

EXECUTED this ________________________.

____
SON SAMPLE

STATE OF ______________________
COUNTY OF ______________________

The foregoing instrument was acknowledged before me this _______ day of ________________________ 20______, by **SON SAMPLE**, who is personally known to me or who has produced ________________________, as identification and who did not take an oath.

____
Notary Public

Seal and Commission
Expiration Stamp

A beneficiary may waive the Trustee's statutory duty to provide accountings

Figure 17 Trustee's Accounting

TRUSTEE'S ACCOUNTING OF THE SAMPLE LIVING TRUST DATED FEBRUARY 1, 1999
from January 12, 2017 though December 31, 2017

The purpose of this accounting is to acquaint all interested persons with the transactions that have occurred during the period covered by the accounting and the assets that remain on hand. It consists of a SUMMARY sheet and Schedule A showing all Receipts, Schedule B showing all Disbursements, Schedule C showing all Distributions, Schedule D showing all Capital Transactions and Adjustments (the effect of which are also reflected in other schedules, if appropriate), and Schedule E showing assets on hand at the end of the accounting period.

It is important that this accounting be carefully examined. Requests for additional information and any questions should be addressed to the Trustee, the name and address is set forth below.

Under penalties of perjury, the undersigned Trustee declares that I have read and examined this accounting and that the facts and figures set forth in the Summary and the attached Schedules are true, to the best of my knowledge and belief, and that it is a complete report of all cash and property transactions and of all receipts and disbursements of THE SAMPLE LIVING TRUST DATED FEBRUARY 1, 1999, from January 12, 2017, through December 31, 2017.

Signed on ______________, _____.

Trustee:

____

DAUGHTER SAMPLE
123 Government Street
Pensacola, FL 32502

Pursuant to Florida Statute 736.1008, an action for breach of trust based on matters disclosed in a trust accounting or other written report of the trustee may be subject to a 6-month statute of limitations from the receipt of the trust accounting or other written report. If you have questions, please consult your attorney.

This letter gives a brief description of the accounting documents and advises the beneficiary to contact the Trustee with any questions.

Figure 17 Trustee's Accounting (continued)

TRUSTEE'S ACCOUNTING OF THE SAMPLE LIVING TRUST DATED FEBRUARY 1, 1999
from January 12, 2017 though December 31, 2017

SUMMARY

	Income	Principal	Totals
I. Starting Balance/ Date of Death Inventory			$315,000.00
II. Receipts			
Schedule A:	$0.00	$10,000.00	$10,000.00
III. Disbursements			
Schedule B:	$0.00	($800.00)	($800.00)
IV. Distributions			
Schedule C:	$0.00	($20,000.00)	($20,000.00)
V. Capital Transactions and Adjustments			$15,000.00
Schedule D: Net Gain or (Loss)			
VI. Assets on Hand at Close of Accounting Period			
Schedule E: Cash and Other Assets			$319,200.00

The Summary gives an overview of the debits and credits of the Trust estate during the specified period.

Figure 17 Trustee's Accounting (continued)

TRUSTEE'S ACCOUNTING OF THE SAMPLE LIVING TRUST DATED FEBRUARY 1, 1999
from January 12, 2017 though December 31, 2017

SCHEDULE A - RECEIPTS

Date	Brief Description of Items	Income	Principal
4/6/2016	Insurance policy proceeds		$10,000.00
	Total Income & Principal	**$0.00**	**$10,000.00**

The Receipts Schedule details all payments received by the Trust.

Figure 17 Trustee's Accounting (continued)

TRUSTEE'S ACCOUNTING OF THE SAMPLE LIVING TRUST DATED FEBRUARY 1, 1999
from January 12, 2017 though December 31, 2017

SCHEDULE B - DISBURSEMENTS

Date	Brief Description of Items	Income	Principal
02/11/16	Trust attorney fees		($800.00)
	Total Disbursements	**$0.00**	**($800.00)**

The Disbursements Schedule details all expenses paid by the Trust.

Figure 17 Trustee's Accounting (continued)

TRUSTEE'S ACCOUNTING OF THE SAMPLE LIVING TRUST DATED FEBRUARY 1, 1999
from January 12, 2017 though December 31, 2017

SCHEDULE C - DISTRIBUTIONS

Date	Brief Description of Items	Income	Principal
3/9/2016	Partial distribution to Daughter Sample		($10,000.00)
3/9/2016	Partial distribution to Son Sample		($10,000.00)
	Total Distributions	**$0.00**	**($20,000.00)**

The Distributions Schedule details all transfers made the beneficiaries of the Trust.

Figure 17 Trustee's Accounting (continued)

TRUSTEE'S ACCOUNTING OF THE SAMPLE LIVING TRUST DATED FEBRUARY 1, 1999
from January 12, 2017 though December 31, 2017

SCHEDULE D - CAPITAL TRANSACTIONS AND ADJUSTMENTS

Date	Brief Description of Transactions	Net Gain	Net Loss
11/15/2016	Increase in homestead property value	$15,000.00	
	Total Net Gains and (Losses)	**$15,000.00**	**$0.00**
	Net Gain or (Loss)		**$15,000.00**

The Capital Transactions and Adjustment Schedule details any gains or losses in the value of a Trust asset.

Figure 17 Trustee's Accounting (continued)

TRUSTEE'S ACCOUNTING OF THE SAMPLE LIVING TRUST DATED FEBRUARY 1, 1999
from January 12, 2017 though December 31, 2017

SCHEDULE E - ASSETS ON HAND AT CLOSE OF ACCOUNTING PERIOD

	Estimated Current Value	Carrying Value
ASSETS OTHER THAN CASH:		
Homestead property	$265,000.00	$265,000.00
Other Assets Total:	**$265,000.00**	**$265,000.00**
CASH:		
Credit Union		$54,200.00
Cash Total:		**$54,200.00**
TOTAL ASSETS (must agree with the Total for Item VI on Summary)		**$319,200.00**

The Assets on Hand at Close of Accounting Period Schedule details all those assets remaining in the Trust at the end of the specified period.

Figure 18 No Objection to Annual/Final Accounting

NO OBJECTION TO ANNUAL/FINAL ACCOUNTING
JANUARY 12, 2017 - DECEMBER 31, 2017

IN RE: **THE SAMPLE LIVING TRUST DATED FEBRUARY 1, 1999**

The undersigned, **SON SAMPLE**, does hereby:

1. Acknowledge I am fully aware of my rights as a beneficiary of the above named Trust under Florida Law, as those rights relate to the Trustee's duties of accounting.

2. Acknowledge I am in receipt of and have reviewed the annual accounting for **THE SAMPLE LIVING TRUST DATED FEBRUARY 1, 1999**.

3. Pursuant to Florida Statute 736.1012 and the Florida Trust Code, I hereby consent to the accounting and have no objections to the accounting. I further release, discharge and agree to hold harmless **DAUGHTER SAMPLE**, from any further accountability and liability in connection with said accounting.

This the ______________ day of ________________, 20____.

____
SON SAMPLE, Beneficiary

Signed by a beneficiary to acknowledge they have received the final accounting of the Trust and have no objections to the information provided

Figure 19 Final Waiver, Receipt, Release and Refunding Agreement

FULL AND FINAL DISTRIBUTION
WAIVER, RECEIPT, RELEASE AND REFUNDING AGREEMENT

IN RE: **THE SAMPLE LIVING TRUST DATED FEBRUARY 1, 1999**

The undersigned, **SON SAMPLE**, does hereby:

1. Acknowledge that **DAUGHTER SAMPLE**, Trustee of the above referenced Trust, has delivered the following property to the undersigned, **SON SAMPLE**, beneficiary of **THE SAMPLE LIVING TRUST DATED FEBRUARY 1, 1999**:

    - **$138,040 (ONE HUNDRED THIRTY-EIGHT THOUSAND FORTY DOLLARS)**

2. Acknowledge the above-described property as final distribution from the Trust.

3. Release, discharge, and agree to hold harmless **DAUGHTER SAMPLE**, from any further accountability and liability in connection with said property.

4. Agree, in consideration of the delivery of said property, that if any claims, and fiduciaries' compensation become properly payable by the Trustee out of the said property, the undersigned will, immediately upon demand, pay over the amount thereof to the Trustee or retransfer and redeliver to the Trustee for sale and liquidation such part of the said property as the Trustee shall demand.

5. Release and discharge **DAUGHTER SAMPLE** from any further administrative duties and responsibilities and/or liability for further administration of the Trust.

6. Waive **DAUGHTER SAMPLE's** duty to provide the undersigned with future accountings as set forth under Florida Statute 736.0813(1)(d).

This the ______________ day of ________________, 20____.

____
SON SAMPLE, Beneficiary

Signed by a beneficiary to acknowledge they have received final distribution of their share from the Trustee